THE
BANK OF ENGLAND
NOTE

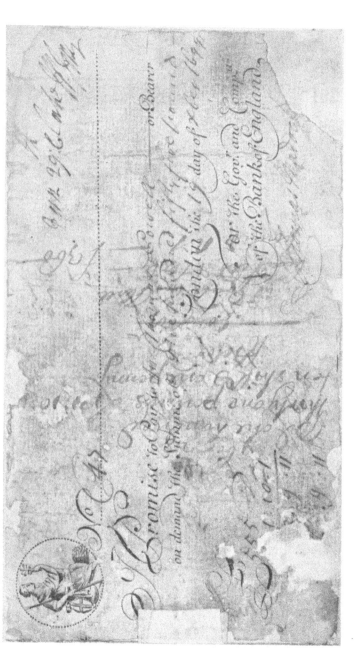

The earliest existing printed Bank of England note to bearer.
Actual size $4\frac{1}{2}$ in. $\times 7\frac{3}{4}$ in.

THE
BANK OF ENGLAND NOTE

A HISTORY OF ITS PRINTING

BY

A. D. MACKENZIE

CAMBRIDGE
AT THE UNIVERSITY PRESS
1953

CAMBRIDGE UNIVERSITY PRESS
Cambridge, New York, Melbourne, Madrid, Cape Town, Singapore,
São Paulo, Delhi, Dubai, Tokyo, Mexico City

Cambridge University Press
The Edinburgh Building, Cambridge CB2 8RU, UK

Published in the United States of America by
Cambridge University Press, New York

www.cambridge.org
Information on this title: www.cambridge.org/9780521172073

First published 1953
First paperback printing 2010

A catalogue record for this publication is available from the British Library

ISBN 978-0-521-17207-3 Paperback

PREFACE

MUCH HAS been written on the subject of the history and activities of the Bank of England, and although in these works due regard has been paid to the notes issued by the Bank, no work dealing with the Bank of England note *per se* has, up to the present, appeared. In the following pages, the preparation of which has been undertaken at the request of the Bank of England, an attempt has been made to fill this gap.

The greater part of the material from which these pages were compiled has been derived from the Bank's records and those at St Luke's Printing Works. The collection of Bank of England notes in the Issue Office of the Bank has been consulted extensively, and has proved an invaluable guide to the changing face of the note throughout the centuries. The value of this collection is greatly enhanced by the profuse annotations of Thomas Zwinger, who collated and arranged these notes, and to whose work in this field I am greatly indebted. Throughout the whole of this research I received the most generous help and co-operation, and I am glad to have this opportunity of expressing my thanks to the officials and staffs of the departments concerned, who have spared no effort to further my investigations and make smooth my path.

Much information has been derived from the consultation of published works, a list of which will be found at the end of this volume. Outstanding among these is *The Bank of England from Within*, by W. Marston Acres, a work which not only provides a mine of information on the Bank in general, but also serves as a guide, by means of which the seeker after the particular may more readily follow his special line of investigation. In the pursuit of the printed word, recourse has been had to a number of libraries, not only the great national collections and those of municipalities, but also the libraries of several institutions and societies who have been so good as to allow me to have access to their shelves. An abundant harvest, too, has been gathered from the museums. Apart from its indispensable library, the British Museum has contributed greatly to the success of my research, as have also the Victoria and Albert Museum and the Science Museum. I am greatly indebted, too, to a number of firms and private individuals who took infinite pains to secure for me information, in regard to which I had written to them.

The completed copy of this work was read by Professor R. S. Sayers, by my one-time chief, H. G. de Fraine, and by my former colleagues, S. B. Chamberlain and J. R. Dudin, to each of whom I am indebted for a number of materially helpful suggestions. To these and to the officials and staffs of the libraries and museums concerned, as well as to the firms and private individuals referred to above, I am deeply grateful for the help that I have received.

A. D. MACKENZIE

London
September 1952

CONTENTS

LIST OF PLATES

CHAPTER I

THE FIRST CENTURY OF THE BANK OF
ENGLAND NOTE

IN LONDON, towards the middle of the seventeenth
century, the merchants had, for the best of reasons,
lost their confidence in the Tower as a place of safe
deposit, and the custom had grown up of depositing bullion or valuables for safe custody with the Goldsmiths,
who would give receipts for the sums deposited. Later,
these receipts embodied a promise to repay, and, finally,
took the form of promissory notes. They were known as
Goldsmiths' notes, and were used for the purpose of
making payments among merchants. When the deposit
consisted of the depositor's 'running cash', that is to say,
cash that should be immediately available for use, a proportion had, again, to be kept by the Goldsmiths as their
running cash, against the presentation of the notes for
payment, which might be either in part or in whole. If in
part, a record of the transaction would be made upon the
face of the note, and its value reduced to the amount of the
outstanding balance. So convenient was this custom to
the public, and so profitable to the Goldsmiths, that in
1677 there were in London no less than forty-four Goldsmiths, who kept running cashes. The Goldsmiths' notes
were, at this time, entirely in manuscript, and as their
circulation was very limited, at no time did they serve the
purpose of a general note issue. When the Bank of England
was founded in 1694, there were a number of bankers
operating throughout Europe, but none of these were

banks of issue, so that the notes, then issued by the Bank, were, with one exception, the first of their kind. The exception referred to was the issue by the Bank of Sweden, in 1661, of notes which were the first actual bank-notes to be issued in Europe.[1]

The Swedish notes were printed documents for specific amounts, with the number and date added in manuscript. The issue was an immediate success, and the notes even went to a premium, compared with the coinage. This effect was probably due to the fact that the coinage, based on a copper standard, was extremely cumbersome; the ten dollar coin, for example, weighed 19.7 kilos—the heaviest coin ever known—so that the payment of anything greater than the smallest of sums necessitated the use of heavy transport. In the short space of two years, however, the currency principle came into play; copper money flowed out of the country, and the Bank of Sweden had difficulty in cashing the notes presented for payment. There was, therefore, no alternative but to discontinue the issue, which came to an end in 1664, three years after its inception.[2]

Although the Swedish notes were the first actual bank-notes, they were by no means the first issue of notes of any kind. This event had taken place nearly a thousand years previously, when the earliest paper currency of which there is any record is said to have been issued by the Chinese in the seventh century under the T'ang Dynasty. Issues of notes continued to be made under subsequent dynasties, and, as might be expected, were not without their difficulties, for we find that, in the year 1000, it became necessary to promulgate a decree to the effect that

[1] Sir John Clapham, *The Bank of England: A History*, vol. I, p. 3.
[2] E. F. Heckscher, *The Bank of Sweden* (quoted in J. G. van Dillen, *History of the Principal Public Banks*, p. 169).

only the Government should issue notes, and in 1300 we hear of a protest by merchants at the inflationary effect of an over-issue. Nevertheless this form of currency must have proved a success, for it continued to circulate until it was discontinued in the fifteenth century under the Ming Dynasty.

Marco Polo, during the seventeen years of his residence in China, had been greatly impressed by the idea, as he put it, of 'paper cut into pieces of money', and in the account of his travels, written in 1298, he gives a description of the notes that were then in circulation under the Great Khan Kublai. From it we learn that they were printed in black ink on the peculiarly dark grey paper produced by pulping the bark of the mulberry tree, and bore the authorising seals in bright vermilion. He writes enthusiastically of the convenience of this medium of exchange, giving instances of its utility for the settlement of internal transactions, and even goes so far as to approve of its suitability as a means of paying for imports.[1] It is, however, remarkable that he makes no mention of the art of printing, by which the notes were produced. Such mention might have expedited the introduction of printing in the West by more than a hundred years, for it was not until the middle of the fifteenth century that both plate-printing and surface or letterpress printing were invented in Europe. As we shall be concerned later with both of these methods, it may be as well to explain briefly that plate-printing is the production of a printed impression on paper from a design previously engraved in recess on a metal plate. The plate is inked, cleaned and polished, the

[1] Marco Polo tells, with some naïveté, how the merchants, who brought their caravans to Peking with goods for sale, could have no objection to being paid in paper money, as they might, if they were inhabitants of a country where this paper was not current, invest it in the purchase of goods suited to their own markets!

ink remaining only in the incised lines, so that the paper, previously damped, when brought into contact with the plate under very heavy pressure, is forced into the incisions, and thus produces the impression. Letterpress or surface printing is effected by means of type or blocks in relief, the face only of which is inked, the impression being produced by contact with the paper under a firm but comparatively light pressure.

It is a matter for surprise that Marco Polo's Venetian contemporaries who were bankers were not inspired by his eulogies of a paper currency. Nevertheless, no attempt would appear to have been made, even after the coming of printing, to issue a bank-note, which would form an everyday currency, until the issue by the Bank of Sweden in the seventeenth century, thirty years before the foundation of the Bank of England.

The earliest depositors with the Bank of England had the choice of three methods by which they might obtain repayment. The amount of the deposit might be entered in a book or on a sheet, and drawn upon by the depositor, or he might be given an 'accomptable note' in the form of a receipt for his deposit, upon which he could draw. By the third method, he would receive notes payable to bearer, which, like the Goldsmiths' notes, could, if required, be cashed only in part, and it is this document, described by Sir John Clapham as the bank-note *par excellence*, with which we are concerned, and whose history we are to follow.

The very first notes issued by the Bank were written by hand, aided perhaps by a few lines of engraving, for proofs exist at St Luke's Printing Works—the name given to the printing department of the Bank of England when it moved from the Bank to premises in Old Street, occupied until 1916 by St Luke's Hospital—of a plate engraved with the words 'I promise to pay unto   on demand' at the head, and 'For the Governor and Company of the Bank of England' at the foot, but there is no evidence that these plates were ever used, for existing examples of the earliest notes are entirely in manuscript. On 31 July 1694, however, four days after the sealing of the Charter, the Court of Directors ordered 'that the Running Cash Notes be printed'. The method to be employed was plate-printing, and copper plates were engraved for notes of £5, £10, £20, £50 and £100. Proofs of these plates also are in the possession of St Luke's Printing Works, and from them we learn that three notes of the same denomination, each $4\frac{2}{5}$ inches by $8\frac{1}{5}$ inches were engraved on one plate, and that they were lettered in accordance with their denomination. The following is a transcript of the £5 note.

	Vignette of Britannia	
A		No...............

We promise to pay Mr...or Bearer

the Sum of five pounds at demand, London the .... } £5

day of .... 169......

Ent'd   for the Govr. & Company of the
                                         Bank of England

This Note to be currant only for twelve months and may be checked at the Bank gratis when desired.

The notes of other denominations were identical, except for changes in the distinguishing letter, and in the design of the vignette and of the border surrounding it.

The figure of Britannia, which formed the subject of the vignette, had been adopted by the Bank as their seal, when on 30 July 1694 the Court of Directors ordered 'that the Seale which was now shewn to this Court . . . being Britannia sitting and looking on a Bank of mony . . . be the Common Seale of the Company in all their transactions'. The figure resembles very closely the design by John Roettier, which appeared on the reverse of the copper halfpenny of 1672, and which embodied the characteristics of the original Britannia,created by the Emperor Hadrian for use on the coinage of Britain in the first century A.D. The figure is bareheaded—originally to distinguish it from the helmeted figure of Roma—and is armed with a spear, while the left hand holds an olive branch. In the Bank's version, the shield is fittingly emblazoned with the Cross of St George, instead of the 'old' Union Flag,[1] which appears on the coin of 1672, and the 'Bank of mony' is represented by a pile of coins at the side of the figure. This vignette of Britannia, which, in the course of years, has taken varying forms, has been a feature of every printed Bank of England note, from the very beginning until the present day.

There can be little doubt that notes printed from these plates were never issued, for on 6 August 1694 the Court of Directors decided that: 'The Notes for Running Cash being considered liable to be counterfeited, for preventing thereof it was ordered that they be done on marbled paper Indented.'[2] In the absence of any surviving specimen, it is not possible to know the exact appearance of these notes. Research has failed to reveal any contemporary indenture so protected, but it seems probable that the notes were on the same plan as that of an indented cheque, dated 1776, which is reproduced in illustration of an article on 'Tallies', by H. G. de Fraine in *The Old Lady of Threadneedle Street* for March 1924.[3] This cheque was separated from its

[1] That is to say, the flag as it was before the introduction of the saltire of St Patrick in 1801.

[2] Marbled paper: paper marked with streaks and whorls of colour, familiar from its use for the end-papers of books, etc.

[3] Vol. II, no. 13, Plate I, Fig. 4, following p. 184.

No. A

We promise to pay to Mr
five pounds at demand, London the
day of   169

Enter'd

or bearer the Sum of } £ 5.

for the Govr. & Company of the
Bank of England

This Note to be Currant only for twelve months
And may be Checked at the Bank gratis whensoever

II. Proof of a proposed £5 note engraved in 1694.
Actual size 4⅔ in. × 8⅕ in.

counterfoil by the usual elaborate scrollwork, at the back of which a narrow margin of paper had been marbled, and through which the indenting line would be cut. This practice was an invaluable aid to the detection of forgery, for, since no two pieces of marbled paper are exactly alike, the continuity of the design would provide a means of identification, additional to the indentation, when the document was assembled with its counterpart. As for the text, we learn that it was identical with that of the above-mentioned proofs, with the addition of the words 'of this indented Note' after the word 'Bearer', and that, again like the proofs, the notes were printed 'with the forme of the Common Seale on Topp'.

The deliberations on the subject of the new issue were protracted, for it was not until 5 June 1695 that an order was placed for 12,000 of these notes to be 'printed and laid up as Running Cash'. There were seven denominations, and each bore a distinguishing letter. The £5 notes were to be lettered 'A'; £10 'B'; £20 'C'; £30 'D'; £40 'E'; £50 'F'; £100 'G'. It would seem that the printing was carried out by William Staresmore, the Bank's stationer, who had also engraved the necessary plates, for on 2 May 1695 it was ordered 'that the coppers for the printing of the Bank Bills[1] and Bank Notes bee taken up from Mr. Staresmore and delivered to the Committee in Waiting,[2] to be sealed up and laid in the Vault', and on the same date as that of the order to print—for which purpose the plates would have been released—it was directed that the 'Copper

[1] Bank bills were issued from the earliest days; they are first mentioned on 30 July 1694. The Bank's seal was affixed to each bill, and they were consequently known as Bank bills sealed, or sealed bills.

[2] The Committee in Waiting was first appointed on 28 July 1694, when a rota of Directors was instituted, from which five directors (the number was subsequently reduced) were required to attend at the Bank in the intervals between the meetings of the Court of Directors, for the transaction of day-to-day business.

Plates of the old and new Bank Notes be brought in and locked up in the Treasury soe soon as they are all printed off'. The issue was short-lived for, in August of the same year, a forged note for £100 was presented for payment, and on the fourteenth of that month it was ordered 'that all the Running Cash Notes for the future be written by some of the Cashiers, and that noe more of the printed ones bee delivered out'.

No time was lost in seeking a remedy, for a week later it was decided that a 'mould be made for making Ten reames of paper', and a special committee was appointed to 'consider of the forme of the Mould'. Thus the idea of a special watermark, which thenceforward was to be an outstanding feature of all Bank of England notes, first came about. Its development, however, took some time. In December of the same year, the making of a 'peculiar[1] sort of paper' was considered, but it was not until March 1697 that Alexander Merrial, who had carried out the work, was paid for the manufacture of 'paper frames', and it was decided to 'make paper upon them'. The work was entrusted to Rice Watkins of Sutton Courtenay in Berkshire, who lost no time in proceeding with the making, for less than a month later the Bank's representative, Conrad de Golse, was sent down to the mills to 'see the paper worked off', and by July 1697—four months later—some of the paper had been received by the Bank. Not soon enough, however, for it to be used for the earliest examples of printed notes now in the Bank's possession. These are printed upon plain paper and are dated June 1697: they are not notes to bearer, but accomptable notes, that is to say, deposit receipts, with a promise to repay.

The paper was made, as was all paper of good quality at that time, from linen rag, with perhaps a proportion of

[1] That is to say, a sort of paper peculiar to the Bank.

III. The paper mill at Sutton Courtenay, Berkshire

printing of the running cash notes was resumed at the same time; nevertheless, the oldest existing specimen of a note to bearer is dated no earlier than 19 December 1699. This note is extremely frail and, for its better preservation, has been pasted on a thick sheet of paper. The watermark is consequently hardly discernible, but on other notes of the same year it can be seen that the design of the watermark consisted of a looped border with an elaborate scroll in the dexter[1] margin, and a panel, bearing the words 'Bank of England' in italic capitals near the foot of the note. The following is a transcript of this note, which measures $4\frac{1}{2}$ inches by $7\frac{3}{4}$ inches; italic characters indicate that the words and figures thus shown were in manuscript.

Vignette
of
Britannia
No. *47*
I promise to pay to *Mr Thomas Powell* or Bearer on demand the summe of *Five hundred fifty five pounds*

£*555*

London the *19* day of *Xber 1699*
for the Govr. and Comp^a.
of the Bank of England
Thomas Madockes

Reference to the frontispiece—a facsimile of this note—will show that it was paid in three instalments, £131 10*s*. 1*d*., £360 and finally the balance of £63 9*s*. 11*d*.

It will be seen that the vignette had been moved to the top dexter corner, where it has remained until the present day, and that the printing of notes of varying denomina-

[1] It was not until the year 1809 that the Court of Directors decided that the two halves of a note should be referred to as if they formed part of a heraldic achievement, that is to say that the dexter half is that on the spectator's left hand, and the sinister on his right. In order to avoid confusion, however, this nomenclature will be followed throughout.

tions had been discontinued. The amount, in both words and figures, was added in manuscript by the issuing cashier, and in accordance with an Order of 1696, this amount was never to be less than £50. The number and date were also written by hand. The date was that of the day upon which the note was issued, and the numbers, which were entered in the 'Note Book', as the Register was then called, started at '1' each morning and ran on until the end of the day. Here and there, among remaining specimens, we find a letter adjoining the number. It did not function as does the modern cipher, but was used, it is thought, as a means of identification, when more than one Note Book was in use. Another change worth noticing is the fact that, while the word 'Governor' was, as in the early proofs, abbreviated to Govr by the method usually employed today, the word 'Company' was also abbreviated and, by a more antiquated method, became 'Comp^a'— the 'a' being the next vowel following the abbreviation.[1]

Two notes were engraved, side by side, on each copper plate, and after printing, they were separated by cutting, so that every note had three deckle edges and one cut edge. The printing was carried out on a copperplate press, a form of rolling press capable of producing the very heavy pressure, which, as we have already noted, was required in order to force the paper into the lines engraved on the plate. It is doubtful if any piece of machinery has changed less than this form of press, which was invented in 1545— very early in the history of engraving—and which exists in the same form today, when it is still used for pulling proofs and small editions of engravings and etchings, as it was in

[1] There is no foundation for the popular belief, the origin of which is attributed to Samuel Butler, that the abbreviation 'Comp^a' was, on account of the fact that early banking in this country was in the hands of Lombards, a contraction of the Italian 'Compagnia'.

the seventeenth century when the first Bank of England notes were printed upon it. The press, as will be seen from Plate IV, is a simple affair in which a flat bed is made to slide horizontally between two cylinders. The top cylinder is adjustable so as to secure the correct pressure, and terminates at one end in the cross, a capstan-like fitting by which the cylinder may be rotated. The engraved plate, previously warmed in order that the ink may be kept in a semi-fluid state, is inked, wiped and finally polished by the palm of the pressman's hand, which has been lightly dusted with whitening. The plate, which is then free from ink except in the engraved lines, is laid upon the bed of the press with the paper, previously damped, upon it, covered with a thick blanket and rolled beneath the pressure of the top cylinder. By this means an impression is produced on the paper, which varies in intensity in accordance with the amount of ink in the engraved lines; the printed lines are darker and stronger where the plate is deeply engraved and lighter where the engraving is shallow, giving a liveliness and depth to the finished work that is not possible with any other method of printing. The process is a slow one, but the expert would make little of it, and a good man would print a ream in four hours, that is to say, one sheet—two notes—in half a minute. The turning of the cross demanded considerable exertion, and a pressman had, therefore, to be not only skilful but also physically strong in order to stand the strain of a day's work. As this process continued to be employed for more than 140 years, there is little to record in regard to the actual method of printing, but there were a number of changes affecting the printer that must be mentioned.

During the first few years, several variations were made in the design of the vignette. The olive branch soon lost any resemblance to that of the original design, and showed

IV. The copper-plate press

side-shoots with disk-like terminations, representing, it has been suggested, a sprig of the plant popularly known as honesty. The pile of coins, representing the 'bank of mony', had gradually become more tidy until it resembled a beehive, into which it finally developed. In 1702, John Sturt, noted for his skill in engraving vignettes and text,[1] was engaged to engrave the notes, and a particularly pleasing vignette by him appeared in 1703. But the desire for change seems to have persisted, for Sturt engraved two new versions, one in 1707 and another in 1712. In 1724 the year of issue was engraved immediately below the vignette, which in the following years began gradually to take on a new form, wherein the figure was reduced in size, and subordinated to a conventional foliated border. In 1732 the border was surmounted by a representation of the crown, a feature which has outlasted a great many subsequent changes and still occupies the same position on the notes of the present day. In 1743, the figures denoting the year were removed from below the vignette and placed one half on each side of it, while the border, elaborated more and more during the preceding years, achieved a form which, with only minor changes, remained constant for more than a century. During the years that saw these changes in the design and treatment of the vignette, the form of the text had been gradually changing; the rather tight italic of the earliest notes had, little by little, become more flowing, and during the succeeding years developed into the bank-note script that we know today.

Forgery, as might be expected, was a constant source of trouble. By an Act of 1697, the forgery or alteration of a bank-note was declared to be 'a felony without benefit of

---

[1] The work by which he is chiefly remembered is his *Book of Common Prayer*, published in 1717, which was printed from engraved silver plates.

clergy'.[1] The concluding words would appear to have been highly necessary, for it seems unlikely that any person capable of forgery would be unable to read and write! The prospect of capital punishment, however, did not seem to deter potential forgers. Counterfeiting continued, while erasure and alteration—it will be remembered that the words and figures of the amount were in manuscript— were a constant source of anxiety. In 1722 the Bank, with a view to finding a means of combating this form of crime, adopted the unusual course of sending a cashier to Newgate in order to interview a forger, who had been found guilty of erasing and altering a bank-note, and had been sentenced to death. The condemned man, who was young and well educated, was found to be co-operative, and provided some useful information. He suggested, for example, that erasure would be made practically impossible if the amount of a bank-note were to 'appear on the reverse of the note in figures against the figures on the front', and it is interesting to note that, although no action was taken at the time, this very device was tried, nearly a hundred years later, as a security measure.

The Bank, however, concentrated more particularly on the forger's criticism of the paper, which he declared to be spongy and ill-coloured so that it contributed to the success of erasure by chemicals.[2] Now the bank-note paper was still manufactured at Sutton Courtenay Mill, where Rice Watkins, who had died in 1705, had been succeeded by Thomas Napper, who now conducted the business, and although the paper appeared to be in no way inferior

[1] Benefit of clergy, by which clerks in holy orders were exempt from capital punishment, had been extended in 1350 to any who could read or write. It was abolished in 1827.

[2] W. Marston Acres, *The Bank of England from Within*, p. 122. The prisoner's sentence was shortly afterwards commuted to transportation for life.

to that originally supplied, it must be assumed that the Bank were anxious to secure something better. It was at this time that the Governor of the Bank, Sir Gilbert Heathcote, heard, through his nephew William Heathcote of Hursley in Hampshire, of a Huguenot friend of his, Henry Portal, who some years before had been a neighbour of the Heathcotes during the time that he had been engaged in the manufacture of paper with a community of fellow Huguenots, the founders and proprietors of the 'Company of White Paper Makers in England', at South Stoneham.[1] Henry Portal had now been for some twelve years engaged in paper-making on his own account at Bere Mill on the River Test near Whitchurch in Hampshire, and with a degree of success that had encouraged him a few years before to acquire a neighbouring corn mill at Laverstoke and to build upon its site another paper mill. He had already a reputation for the excellence of his paper, and it was suggested that he would be able to supply bank-note paper superior to that then in use. The suggestion was considered, with the result that in 1724, after the necessary preliminaries were concluded, the Bank entered into an agreement with Henry Portal for the supply of bank-note paper. Thus began the intimate connection of the Portal family with the Bank, a connection that has lasted until the present day. The new paper was a great improvement upon that previously used. It was harder and of better texture, while the watermark had a definition and clarity not to be found in the old paper. The design of the watermark was unchanged, except that the words 'Bank of England' in the panel at the foot of the note were in roman capitals instead of in italic.

In 1725, as soon as the new paper was in use, it was decided to resume the printing of notes for fixed sums, and

[1] Sir William Portal, *The Story of Portals Ltd. of Laverstoke*, p. 5.

an order was given that copper plates be engraved for notes of £20, £30, £40, £50, and £100. The idea seems to have been carried out only partially, for a note for £50, dated 30 June 1732, shows the amount in words in the text to have been printed, the word 'pounds' being added in manuscript, and in the place reserved for the figures, a printed '£' sign with the first numeral only of the amount, the nought being added by hand. The year 1743, however, saw the beginning of the 'sum piece', an elaborate '£' sign followed by the amount spelt out in white gothic letters on a black ground. This characteristic feature of the Bank of England note has changed comparatively little during the period—more than two hundred years—that has elapsed since its first appearance. The bead-like projections on the border of the black background have become more defined, but the general design has remained much the same. Each denomination[1] had its special pattern, and their intricate scroll-work afforded ample opportunity for the engraver to display his skill in both design and execution. Another feature, which has remained unchanged since it was first printed on the notes for fixed sums, is the amount in words in the text. From its first appearance, this word has been printed in the bold black gothic lettering that has persisted throughout the years, and still forms an outstanding feature of the Bank of England note.

During the Seven Years War, a shortage of currency was brought about by the export of specie; in 1759, the Bank, with a view to meeting the shortage, authorised the issue of notes for £10 and £15, and in 1765 notes for £25 were issued. The succeeding twenty years, during which stirring events and epoch-making changes occurred both

[1] In 1745, notes for the following denominations were being printed: £20, £30, £40, £50, £60, £70, £80, £90, £100, £200, £300, £400, £500 and £1000.

V. Bere Mill, near Whitchurch, Hampshire

at home and abroad, were devoid of incident in the history
of the bank-note, which, although the circulation continued to increase, suffered no change until 1782, when it
became the established practice that all notes should be
made payable to the Chief Cashier for the time being. This
practice, which continued for more than seventy years,
has aroused considerable speculation as to the origin of so
curious a procedure, for curious it was that the Bank
should issue notes, signed on its behalf by a junior cashier
and payable to his chief, who would possibly never see
them, while the notes themselves went out to provide the
currency of the country. The series of events that brought
about this practice may be said to have started some years
before the foundation of the Bank, in the complications
that had arisen in connection with the Goldsmiths' notes.
During the latter part of the seventeenth century, many
of the 'Customs of Merchants from Time out of Mind' in
regard to bills of exchange had become part of the common law, but some confusion had arisen as to the negotia-
bility of the Goldsmiths' notes, which were in effect promissory notes. Although a number of decisions had been
given in the Courts on this question, the decisions were
by no means consistent, and merchants and goldsmiths
alike were far from happy about the legal position of such
paper.

The matter was not finally settled until the passing of
an Act of Parliament in 1704, so that, when the Bank of
England decided in 1694 to issue 'notes payable to bearer',
without which, as Sir Theodore Janssen put it, 'the Bank
could not carry on business',[1] it must be assumed that the
best advice was taken in order to ensure that the notes
were in proper form. This form, as we know, provided a
space for the payee's name, in which the issuing cashier

[1] *Sir John Clapham, The Bank of England: A History*, vol. I, p. 3.

would enter that of the depositor who had chosen this method of drawing upon his deposit, or that of a person to whom he wished to make a payment. After a short time, however, it would seem that notes were not always required for making definite payments, for which purpose cheques were beginning to come into use, but were required simply as currency, and might well have been made payable to a fictitious payee. But on one point the law was clear; notes payable to 'X' or bearer were not legally assignable and, consequently, the bearer, if other than the payee, could not sue in his own name. The name of the payee, therefore, became of the greatest importance, and the custom grew up of entering, in the space provided for the payee's name, that of 'persons known to the bank'. From evidence provided by the 'old clearer',[1] we learn that soon after 1700 the names of Edmond Clarke and John Miller, both tellers in the service of the Bank, were used for this purpose, and that as time went on their places were taken by other employees of the Bank, whose names, as payees, occurred more and more frequently.[2]

In 1752, there appears for the first time the name of Daniel Race, who was Chief Cashier jointly with Elias Simes, and during the next few years his name continues to occur from time to time, but from 1759, in which year Daniel Race was appointed sole Chief Cashier, his name appears repeatedly, as do those of his successors until 1782, when this practice was established. From that year, in the space provided for the payee's name there was written the name of Abraham Newland, the Chief Cashier at that time, and in 1798, his name was printed so that it

[1] The clearers were books in which were entered particulars of notes outstanding at the end of an accounting period.

[2] Under the provisions of the Act of 1704, notes payable to 'X' or bearer became assignable, but, as the Bank continued the practice, the name of the payee was evidently still regarded as important.

formed part of the text of the note. Abraham Newland occupied the position of Chief Cashier until 1807, and the continuous appearance of his name as payee for twenty-five years became so intimately associated in the minds of the public with the Bank of England notes that they were popularly referred to as 'Abraham Newlands'.

The fact that the payee's name would be no longer subject to variation made possible a proposal, which was put forward in the following year, that notes should be 'ready made out' in advance, and a store of such notes accumulated, so that, as the recommendation went on to say, 'the business of issuing Bank Notes in the Hall would be transacted with a much greater degree of security, as well as facility, than at present'. This proposal provides interesting evidence that the number and date of notes must have now become as divorced from reality as had the payee's name. The date was no longer the date of issue, and the numbers would run up to a figure that seemed appropriate to the demand for notes of the denomination concerned; a far cry from the time when each day would open with the issue of note No. 1, bearing the actual date of issue. An interesting relic of this phase in the development of the Bank of England note came to light 112 years later, when there was discovered in the Bank-note Library a forgotten packet of notes, dated 1783 and 1798, which had been completed in accordance with this plan and had, for some reason, never been issued.

The crisis of 1793, following the war with the Revolutionary Government of France, occasioned a further shortage of currency, and in order to meet the deficiency the Bank decided to issue notes for £5; thus the 'fiver', the best known of all Bank of England notes, and the only denomination still issued, except for the present-day notes for £1 and 10s., had to wait for nearly one hundred years

before it was found expedient to issue it.[1] As the war
went on, the consequent diminution of the metallic re-
serves of the Bank became more serious, and the loss of
public confidence, occasioned by alarm at the possibility
of invasion, led to a further demand for gold. On 25 February 1797, news of the Fishguard landing[2] reached London. Although the landing was no more than what we
should, in these days, call a 'raid', public imagination conceived of it as the beginning of the large-scale invasion
that they dreaded, and it was thought that a run on the
Bank was inevitable. On the following day, the King
returned from Windsor to attend a special meeting of the
Privy Council, and on the evening of the same day an
Order in Council was issued to announce the restriction
of cash payments. The cessation of payments in cash made
it incumbent upon the Bank to provide the country with
currency, and, with a view to meeting this need, the Bank
decided to issue notes for £1 and £2. The story of these
notes, and all that followed in their train, is a long one,
and will be dealt with in a subsequent chapter.

In 1793, a minor addition had been made to the form of
the notes, namely, the engraving of the word 'BANK' at
the side of the vignette. It would seem that the word was
introduced in order to denote the place of origin, to be
read in conjunction with the date, for it was discontinued
in 1810, when the method of numbering and dating was
changed and the word 'London' appeared in the date-line.
In the same year, the loss of notes resulting from the theft
of mails on the highway had led to the practice of writing

[1] Notes for £5 were included in the plan for the short-lived 'marbled-
paper notes', but it is not known whether they were ever issued.
[2] The landing at Fishguard on the coast of Pembrokeshire was
effected by a small body of French troops under the command of an
Irish-American adventurer, General Tate. It was overcome with little
difficulty by the local militia.

the number on the dexter as well as the sinister half of the notes, so that they might be cut into two pieces and sent by separate mails. This practice had entailed but little change in the printing, but in 1809 machinery was installed to print the numbers, and at the same time to date the notes. This operation was effected by surface-printing, the numbers being overprinted on the plate-printed words 'promise' and 'Bearer' by means of a machine invented by Joseph Bramah. It was early in 1806 that Bramah first approached the Bank and submitted a model of his machine 'constructed for the purpose of printing the Numbers and Dates of Bank Notes with very great facility'. The machine, as will be seen from Plate VI, was contained in a closed box, the top plate being partially cut away to permit the operation of the numbering mechanism which consisted of two units, each of five wheels, spaced at the correct interval for printing the two numbers of a banknote. The type by which the figures were printed, was cast by the firm of Caslon, and it is interesting to note that these same beautifully proportioned figures continued in use on notes of £5 and upwards for 136 years, until they were replaced by the present style of numbering in 1945. The date-line, which was identical with that now in use, printed the date on each half of the note with the word 'London' between the two dates. It was a stereotype, fixed to the top plate of the machine, and was made of separate pieces, so that a date might be changed without the necessity of replacing the whole line.

The first model submitted by Bramah would appear to have been constructed in accordance with his patent of 15 October 1806, which made no provision for moving mechanically the several wheels of the numbering mechanism; they were, in fact, moved by hand with the aid of a wooden skewer. In November 1807, however, he submitted an

c

improved model, in which the wheels printing the unit figures were turned mechanically after each impression by means of cog-wheels, the other wheels being moved, as before, by means of the skewer. A complication arose from the fact that, as the notes were numbered 'No. 1, No. 2' and so on, instead of in the manner to which we are accustomed today (00001 and so on), it was necessary constantly to change the units wheel. Thus the first wheel, when it had printed '9', was turned to '1' and the cog-wheels were moved to the second wheel, which then became the units wheel to print the unit figures of '10, 11, 12' etc., so that when the ten thousands had been printed each wheel had in turn been the units wheel, the other wheels having been turned by hand when necessary. In 1808, the latest model was finally approved and Bramah was asked to make a double machine, by which the two notes printed on one sheet of paper might be numbered and dated simultaneously. Shortly afterwards thirty of these double machines were ordered at a cost of 240 guineas each.[1] There was no doubt as to the success of the innovation. Each machine was capable of numbering and dating up to 2000 notes per day, whereas 400 notes had been the most that one clerk had been able to produce in a day when the numbering and dating had been done by hand.

In the same year it was decided that the countersignature of notes was no longer necessary, and a large number of clerks, who had previously been employed in numbering, dating and countersigning notes—in 1805, there were 84 of them—were thus released for other work, and the notes, completely printed except for the signature, were delivered directly from the printers to the storekeeper for distribution, as they were required, to the issuing cashiers. The name of Henry Hase, the successor to Abraham New-

---

[1] Eight additional machines were acquired in 1814.

VI. Joseph Bramah's numbering and dating press

land, who had retired in 1807, was now printed in the space where his predecessor's name had previously appeared as payee, and a further change in the appearance of the notes was occasioned by the introduction of a heading, 'Bank of England', printed in the lettering that has been familiar to the public ever since. This heading was followed by the year of issue, and the figures denoting the year, previously shown on each side of the vignette, were discontinued. In order to make known the particulars of these changes, a notice was published in the *London Gazette* of 16 October 1809 to the effect that all Bank of England notes would thenceforward read as follows:

BANK OF ENGLAND   18......

I promise to pay to Mr Henry Hase or Bearer on Demand

the Sum of .... Pounds

18 ....   London ....18 ......

For the Governor and Company[1]
of the Bank of England.

£................   A.B.

In 115 years the Bank of England note had undergone many variations, but it had now taken a definite shape that has, with changes from time to time, been maintained until the present day.

[1] Nevertheless, the actual notes still read 'Gov[r] and Comp[a]'

CHAPTER II

NOTES OF OTHER BANKS

W E H A V E followed the development of the Bank of England note until the beginning of the nineteenth century, and, although it is this note which is our special study, the picture would, it is thought, be lacking in background if we did not glance briefly at bank-note production in other parts of the kingdom in its relationship to the notes of the Bank, and to consider events even farther afield that were eventually to influence the Bank of England note.

At the date of the foundation of the Bank, there were throughout the provinces a number of leading merchants, who, because their stability and integrity had earned the confidence of their fellows, had, as successive industries required their services, assumed and carried out the functions of bankers. Banking facilities were provided also by the money scriveners, a branch of the legal profession, who would make loans to, or invest money on behalf of, their clients, and by a number of agents who specialised in the sending of remittances over a widespread area on behalf of their principals. All these would make advances and deal in bills, but at that time there was no question of an issue of notes payable to bearer. In London, the Goldsmiths continued to issue their manuscript notes, and later—the earliest existing specimen is one of Child's dated 1729—these documents were plate-printed. They were, however, only blank forms upon which the essential details were afterwards entered by hand.

After the failure of the Land Bank, the possibility of similar competition in the future was precluded by an Act of Parliament of 1697, under the provisions of which no subsequent organisation was to be allowed by Act of Parliament to practise Banking. It did not, however, prevent the competition of the Sword Blades Company and the Mine Adventurers' Company, who claimed the right to act as bankers, and who proceeded to issue notes. This form of competition was eliminated by the Acts of 1708 and 1709, whereby organisations of more than six persons were prevented from carrying on the business of banking, so that, except for the Goldsmiths and the provincial merchant bankers, who were all either single individuals or family concerns consisting of not more than six persons, the Bank of England enjoyed a monopoly. It is therefore to Scotland, which was not covered by the provisions of these Acts of Parliament, that we look for another bank-note issue, similar to that of the Bank of England.

On the establishment of the Bank of Scotland, in 1695, it was immediately decided to issue bank-notes, and in the following year an issue was made of notes of £5, £10, £20, £50, and £100. Here again, there was rivalry from unauthorised opponents, for, just as the Sword Blades Company and the Mine Adventurers' Company had issued notes in the early days of the Bank of England, so did the African Company in competition with the newly formed Bank of Scotland; the African Company was the short title of 'The Company trading to Africa and the Indies', which had been formed in 1695 with high hopes of rivalling the wealthy East India Company. The competition, however, did not last long; it came to an end after the disaster of the Darien Scheme, and the consequent failure of the African Company which had set that enterprise on foot.[1]

[1] C. A. Malcolm, *The Bank of Scotland*, 1695-1945, pp. 16, 30, 191.

The first notes issued by the Bank of Scotland were printed in London, and the paper is said to have been of French or Dutch origin,[1] but by 1700 the printing was being carried out in Edinburgh, while the paper was obtained from the mills at Braid, near Edinburgh, and at Yester on the River Esk, of the White Paper Company of Scotland, an offshoot of the Company of White Paper Makers in England, with whom Henry Portal had learned the art and mystery of paper-making. By 1723, this Company was unable to continue the supply, and paper for the Bank of Scotland notes was obtained from Richard Watkins, whose mill was at Penicuik, also on the Esk.[2] The notes were plate-printed from engraved copper plates, and at first all the denominations were in the same text, but in 1700, on the discovery of the MacGhie forgeries, which were achieved by the alteration of a number of £5 notes to £50, it was decided to vary the style of the text for each denomination.[3]

It was not until 1704 that the £1 note that has since been so prominent a feature of Scottish currency was issued. The denomination was shown on the face of this note as 'Twelve pounds Scots,' that is to say £1 sterling, and possibly in order to remove any doubt in the minds of the public among whom the notes circulated, this method of showing the denomination persisted for many years after the Union in 1707, when the old Scots currency had ceased to exist. The £1 notes of 1704 were engraved by James Clerk,[4] the engraver to the Edinburgh Mint, and an early example shows them to have been nearly square in shape (5 inches by 5¼ inches), and on paper with a very promi-

[1] W. Graham, *The One Pound Note*, p. 17.

[2] Robert Waterston, *Early Paper Making near Edinburgh*.

[3] Malcolm, *op. cit.* p. 32.

[4] *Ibid.* p. 184.

nent watermark consisting of a border of deep waves with the words 'BANK OF SCOTLAND' in bold roman capitals. There was no vignette and the text was in roman lettering with some words emphasised in italic. The number and the payee's name were in manuscript; the amount and the date were printed. The note was embossed with the Bank's seal, a female figure representing 'Fortune' seated upon a shield blazoned with a saltire, holding in her right hand a cornucopia and in her left hand a thistle. Each note had a counterfoil which was separated from the note proper by a band of elaborately engraved lettering, through which an indenting line might be cut.

When the Royal Bank of Scotland was established in 1727—the monopoly of the Bank of Scotland had expired in 1716 and had not been renewed—notes were issued for £1, £5, £10, £20, £50 and £100. The design of the early notes, which were engraved by Joseph Cave and Richard Cooper, included a vignette of the king's head. We learn that the paper was supplied, as was that of the Bank of Scotland, by Richard Watkins, and that the price of the paper was 2s. 4d. per 100 sheets.[1]

In 1746, the British Linen Company was founded, and, in the following year, issued bank-notes, which were good examples of engraving and displayed a very attractive vignette consisting of a seated female figure. The following years saw the formation of a number of banks. Starting in Glasgow, Aberdeen and Dundee, the movement spread until there were few towns of any importance that had not their own bank whose notes circulated in their locality. Some of these notes were probably produced by local engravers, but many of them were printed in Edinburgh, where later W. H. Lizars and Robert Kirkwood were to specialise in this branch of work.

[1] Neil Munro, *History of the Royal Bank of Scotland*, pp. 33, 46, 62, 63.

In England and Wales, the monopoly of the Bank of England had prevented the formation of great banks similar to those of Scotland, but by the middle of the eighteenth century a number of the merchant bankers of the country towns, whom we have already noted, had developed into recognised banks, each with their own note issue. Among the more prominent were the Smiths of Nottingham, the Lloyds of Birmingham, Stuckey's in Somerset and Gurney's in Norwich, but throughout the country there were many other banks, whose notes provided currency in their own locality, and even farther afield. The notes were, however, still only plate-printed forms to be completed in manuscript, as indeed the Bank of England notes had been in their earliest days. A very early specimen of a note issued in 1736 by the first of these bankers, shows it to be a plain engraved form, the name of the payee, the amount and the date being added in manuscript, while an interesting reminder that the firm was still a family affair is provided by the signature, which runs 'Abell Smith, for Bro, Samuel and Self'.

It was not long, however, before the notes of the country bankers developed into more elaborate documents, and in every instance it would appear that the Bank of England notes were taken as a model. The text was similar, with a vignette in the corner, or occasionally at the head of the note. The paper was sometimes, but not always, watermarked, and the quality was usually excellent, a circumstance which was due to the fact that it was, in many instances, made by Joseph Portal.[1]

The choice of subject for the vignettes was wide and they took a variety of forms; a favourite one was an engraving of a view, usually incorporating an architectural

[1] Henry Portal had died in 1747, and his son Joseph now directed the mill.

feature of the neighbourhood which would be familiar to the public among whom the notes circulated. The coat armour of the town or county concerned, or that of the banker himself frequently formed the subject of the vignette, while sometimes it was an elaborate design of interlaced letters of a highly decorative type. All these varieties gave full scope to the skill of the engravers, in many instances local men, who would have been employed as a matter of course to execute any required piece of engraving. Their work was consistently good, but little is known of them in any other field. Among them, however, we find the name of Bewick as the engraver of notes for the Northumberland Bank, but whether John or his more famous brother Thomas is not clear. If it was Thomas, his work on these notes is a reminder that he was originally a copper-plate engraver, although it was his skill in the development of the art of wood engraving that earned him lasting fame. It would appear that Mark Lambert, who worked with Bewick, also exercised his original calling, for we find notes of the Bank of Newcastle engraved by him. But, as time went on, the tendency grew for the country banks to procure their notes from firms in London which had set up as specialists in bank-note production. One of these was Gale—afterwards Gale & Butler—of Crooked Lane, and we find a particularly well executed note engraved by John Varley in his young days. Other firms were W. Newman of 27 Widegate Street; B. & I. Thorowgood of 49 Cheapside; Peck of 47 Lombard Street and Silvester of 27 The Strand; but the most important was Harry Ashby, who, earlier in the field than any of them, had set up as Ashby & Co. to become the leading bank-note printer of the time, producing notes for a great number of country banks, and, later, for foreign and colonial banks as well.

The shortage of currency in the second half of the eighteenth century, which had led to the issue by the Bank of England of notes for £10, £15, £25 and subsequently £5, was the cause of an outbreak of notes for smaller amounts all over the country. The success of the issues of the now firmly established country banks encouraged a number of shopkeepers and small firms, provided that they had not more than six partners, to form themselves into banks and to issue notes. Many of these firms had a sound financial basis and the notes performed their functions admirably, but the opening afforded to less reputable organisations had led to the circulation throughout the country of a great many worthless notes. Many of these were well engraved and printed, thereby inspiring confidence in the trusting public, who accepted them, and who suffered accordingly when the 'bank' concerned stopped payment. Many writers have commented upon the evils of this disastrous movement in measured terms, but the words of an anonymous sufferer of the time, that 'any adventuring swindler, who could afford to pay for the engraving of a copper plate, set up a bank' probably represented the opinion of a great many poor people, who had lost what were to them considerable sums of money. The offending notes were, however, mostly for small sums, and two Acts of Parliament passed in 1775 and 1777, which forbade the issue of notes for less than £1 and £5 respectively, did much to end the trouble.

A similar movement was going on in Scotland, but it is to that country that we have to look for a most barefaced attempt to float an issue of notes with no financial backing whatever. In the spring of 1746, Prince Charles Edward Stuart, the Young Pretender, found himself with an empty treasury, which it was proposed to replenish by an issue of notes. The chief item of interest attaching to these notes is that they were engraved—or rather etched, for he had no engraving tools with him on active service—by Robert Strange, who was at that time an officer in the Jacobite army, and who, in later years, as Sir Robert Strange,[1] was to become one of the leading engravers of his day, with a European reputation. Strange, in his *Memoirs*, tells of the difficulties of his task; nevertheless, he submitted his proofs to the Prince and was ready to begin printing on 13 April. The notes were, however, never printed, for three days later the battle of Culloden took place, and with it ended not only this amazing attempt to provide an entirely unbacked currency but also the last hopes of the Jacobite cause.

The Bank of Ireland was founded in 1783. It was late in the day compared with the national Banks of England and Scotland, and the country was already provided with numerous private banks, each with its own note issue, but as soon as the Bank was founded it was decided to issue notes. There were to be sixteen denominations, of varying amounts from £10 to £500, and a director of the Bank came over to this country, in order to arrange with Joseph Portal for the supply of paper. The first notes were, apparently, printed in London, but the bank then decided to take the engraving into their own hands, and George Terry, an engraver of London, was employed to implement this plan.[2] Nothing is known of George Terry, but it is likely that he was of the same family as Garnet Terry, an engraver of Paternoster Row, who had for some years before been employed, from time to time, by the Bank of

---

[1] In 1787 his youthful Jacobite activities had apparently been forgotten, for in that year he was awarded the honour of knighthood by George III.

[2] F. G. Hall, *The Bank of Ireland*, 1783-1946, p. 53.

word, as engraving or etching on steel or iron had been known and practised in the time of Albrecht Dürer, but had fallen into disuse. Not only did Perkins revive this branch of the art soon after 1805, but he went further by case-hardening his plate after engraving, with the idea of using the plate, not for printing but as a kind of master plate—he called it his 'check-plate'—from which he could produce any number of printing plates. But the process of transferring an engraving from one plate to another, to the achievement of which he devoted the next years of his life, developed slowly. He perfected his process as far as it had gone, and printed by its means notes for the New England states, while, in this country, J. C. Dyer, an American, who had settled in London and started the business of introducing and furthering the interests of a number of American inventions, took out in 1810 a patent on Perkins's behalf for the 'check-plate'.

At the same time, two events had taken place in New England that were, together with Perkins's transferring process, to have a far-reaching effect upon bank-note production. Cyrus Durand, a prolific inventor, produced a machine whereby lines, both straight and waved, might be ruled upon a printing plate, and Asa Spencer conceived and developed the idea of engraving printing plates by means of the rose engine.[1] This machine is a variety of the ornamental lathe, and derives its name from the rosettes, shaped disks of metal on the mandrel of the lathe, which, as they revolve, come into contact with a fixed pointer, causing the mandrel to move in accordance with the shape of the rosette, and, together with the variation made possible by an eccentric chuck, to produce an infinite number of designs. The rose engine has, in these days, been superseded by the geometrical lathe and Perkins's plate transfer

[1] D. McN. Stauffer, *American Engravers upon Copper and Steel.*

press and Durand's ruling machine by modern improvements, but it is from the inventions of these three pioneers
that there developed the machines now in world-wide use
for the manufacture of plates to be used in the printing of
bank-notes and other security documents.

In 1814 Perkins joined the firm of Murray, Draper,
Fairman & Co. of Philadelphia, where, with the collaboration of his partners, Gideon Fairman and Asa Spencer, he
continued to work upon the perfection of his plate transfer
press, whereby soft steel rollers under very heavy pressure
were made to take up, in relief, the impression from an
engraved steel plate, and, after hardening, to transfer the
original design to any number of plates to be used for
printing. Five years later Perkins and his invention came
to London.

CHAPTER III

THE PRINTING DEPARTMENT OF
THE BANK OF ENGLAND

WE HAVE seen that William Staresmore, stationer to the Bank, was the first engraver and printer of the Bank of England notes, and that in 1702 John Sturt was entrusted with the engraving. In the same year, the printing was given to James Child, who, with Sturt as engraver, continued to produce the notes for the next eighteen years. Sturt, who by that time was sixty-two years of age, then gave up the work, and in 1721 the engraving was taken over by James Cole. In 1731 Child relinquished the printing, and from that date Cole executed both engraving and printing, at a cost, as is shown by an account preserved in the Bank's museum collections, of 9s. per ream. Now James Cole was a well-known engraver and printer of the period, who carried on his business at the sign of 'The Crown' in Great Kirby Street, Hatton Garden. He had engraved a number of book illustrations, the most notable being the plates for Dart's *Canterbury Cathedral*, which work he had also printed and sold in 1726, and in 1742 he was to engrave the plates for the same author's *Westminster Abbey*. But his work was by no means restricted to architectural subjects; many of the plates in these books show his skill in depicting the figure, and a satirical print, 'The World in Masquerade', is a good example of his lighter work. On his death in 1748, he was succeeded in the family business by George Cole, who continued to print the Bank of England notes and was still doing so in 1783, when a fund of information on the subject becomes available. In that year, a special committee was appointed 'to inspect and enquire into the mode and execution of the business as now carried on in the different departments of the Bank', and from the proceedings of this committee as well as from other sources, it is possible to reconstruct the procedure followed at that time throughout the whole process of bank-note production.

The moulds upon which the paper was made, when completed by the Bank's mould-maker Mrs Mary Smith, were kept in safe custody at the Bank and sent to the mills as they were required. The custom, which had started in 1697, of maintaining a representative at the paper mills in order to 'oversee' the making of the paper, had been continued—at the mills he was known as 'the Bank Officer'—and the Bank had rented a house, in which he lived, close to the Mill at Laverstoke. The paper, as soon as its manufacture was completed, was locked in massive iron-bound chests, and dispatched to the Bank by road in Joseph Portal's own wagons. At first, the transit by road had ended at Newbury, and the chests had completed the journey by barge, via the Kennet and Thames, but this practice had been discontinued after the first few years. On arrival at the Bank, the paper was taken over for safe custody by the cashiers, one of whom would, at the beginning of each month, deliver to the printer, 'Mr Cole, of Kirby Street, Hatton Street', the quantity that he deemed sufficient for the month's work. The engraved copper plates were also in the custody of the cashiers, and each morning the plates necessary for the day's work were taken to Great Kirby Street in the dual control of a cashier and a clerk. The former returned to the Bank, while the latter remained at the printer's for the rest of the

D

day, during which he watched the printing and took over the sheets as they came from the presses. After he had counted the sheets, they were hung up to dry, and during that process they remained in the sole custody of the printer. The clerk then returned to the Bank, with the copper plates, while the printer, when sufficient dry sheets were available, counted them into reams, which, when they amounted to ten in number—four or five days' work —were delivered to the Bank. The special committee were apparently satisfied with the measures employed to control the printing process, but they did not approve of the practice of allowing the paper and plates to go out of the Bank,[1] in spite of the fact that this procedure had been followed since the establishment of the Bank, and made a strong recommendation that 'the Notes be printed within this House'.

The recommendation of the special committee was approved, but there was considerable delay in putting it into practice,[2] for it was not until early in 1791 that Cole brought his business within the walls of the Bank. An application made by him in June of that year for the payment of expenses in connection with this move was deferred, but in the following October, when his application was again considered, it was agreed to increase the payment for printing from 15s. to 20s. per ream, and to make him an allowance of £30 per quarter 'as an Indemnification for his extraordinary Trouble and Expense in doing the business at the Bank instead of his own House'. It was, however, still his own business, and he engaged, controlled and dismissed his staff at will, without reference to

[1] With every reason—Great Kirby Street was more than a mile from the Bank, and within a stone's throw of Field Lane, a notorious resort of criminals.

[2] Probably on account of the lack of accommodation; extensive building operations were proceeding during the years concerned.

the authorities of the Bank. At the same time, the Printing
Office was established under the control of the Chief
Cashier, while Mr Hulme, who had been one of the last of
the clerks to make the daily journey to Great Kirby Street,
carried on his old work of supervision and the control of
plates, paper and printing; otherwise the printers operated
independently. The quarters allotted to them were apparently intended to be only temporary, for in the previous
year, Mr Soane (afterwards Sir John Soane), who had
been appointed architect to the Bank in 1788 on the death
of Sir Robert Taylor, had been instructed to prepare plans
for the erection of barracks for the Bank guard, and
'apartments over the same for engraving and printing Bank
Notes'. But the existing barracks, which had been completed only two years previously, must have provided
sufficient accommodation for the guard, for they apparently continued to occupy it,[1] and some seventeen
years were to elapse before the 'apartments' were completed and the Printing Office was able to move to its
permanent quarters at the western end of the Lothbury
frontage of the Bank.

Only four years after the setting up of his business
within the Bank, George Cole died, and, in the following
month, on 5 March 1795, the Committee of Treasury[2]
appointed his brother William Cole, together with Garnet
Terry, to be jointly bank-note engravers and printers to
the Bank. Garnet Terry, whose name we have noted in

[1] It was still occupied by the guard when that portion of the Bank
was pulled down in 1933.

[2] On 23 August 1694 a committee was appointed 'to attend the
Lords of the Treasury'. In the course of time, this committee—
known as the Committee of Treasury—became the Bank's principal
committee. It made recommendations to the Court of Directors
and, on occasion, as in the present instance, took action on its own
authority. It consisted of the Deputy Governor and certain senior
Directors under the chairmanship of the Governor.

connection with the Bank of Ireland, had a long-standing association with the Bank of England, by whom he had been employed from time to time during the previous twenty years, often as a consultant in connection with forgery proceedings. Apart from the jewellers' designs that we have already noted, he had engraved a number of trade cards and plates for the illustration of books, as well as some charming sketch portraits of popular actors of the period.

The principal task of the newly appointed printers was to deal with the steadily increasing production of notes, due to the introduction, two years before, of notes for £5. Appropriate increases had been made in the staff, but the advent of notes for £1 and £2 in 1797 called for a much greater expansion. Before the printers came into the Bank, they had employed three journeymen, who printed about 2000 notes per day, whereas in 1800 the production of £1 and £2 notes alone amounted to some 15,000 per day. Eighteen presses were constantly in use; twenty journeymen were employed,[1] and the printers asked continually for more presses and more space. In 1801, it was apparently thought desirable to confirm the appointment, made by the Committee of Treasury six years before, for on 11 June of that year, the Court of Directors appointed William Cole and Garnet Terry to be engravers and printers of bank-notes and bank post bills.[2] Mr Hulme,

[1] Some of the new employees were not freemen of the City of London, and in 1801 special permission had to be obtained from the Lord Mayor and the Court of Aldermen to regularise this contravention of the privileges of the City.

[2] Sealed bills (see p. 7 n.) were discontinued shortly after 1716. In 1722 the Committee of Treasury was instructed to 'consider of a method to prevent the inconveniences that happen by Robbing the Mails of Bank Notes', and in 1724 the public were advised that 'the Bank do issue Bills of Exchange'. These bills, at three, and later at seven days date, became known as Bank post bills and, as they were less easily negotiated than bank-notes, were entrusted freely to the mails.

who was now head clerk of the Printing Office, with a staff of five clerks, moved to a less exacting position in the Bank, and a successor was appointed in his place.

Two years later, William Cole died, and on the following day Terry made a formal application to be appointed in sole charge of the engraving and printing. In support of his application, he criticised the late regime in the plainest terms and enlarged upon the many disadvantages of a divided command. His contention would appear to have convinced the Court of Directors, for on 26 May 1803 Terry was appointed engraver and printer to the Bank, with J. H. Harper and William Bawtree as assistant and deputy assistant, respectively, it being stipulated that these two assistants should not be removed without the approval of the Court. Otherwise the principle of the private firm was maintained; the Bank supplied presses and the copper required for new plates, while Terry was paid in accordance with the number of plates engraved and reams printed.

By this time, the production of bank-notes was increasing day by day, and particular attention was given to this branch of the Bank's work, with a view to maintaining a high degree of security throughout the process of manufacture. The moulds for paper-making were made in the Bank, and a request from William Brewer, the mould-maker, who had been appointed in 1800, that in order to cope with the increased demand he might be allowed to perform some of the work at home during the evenings was refused. He pointed out that a mould should 'run off' 2000 reams of paper, but that they were so roughly used by the paper-makers that they were constantly in need of repair, with consequent delay to his work on the much needed new moulds. He was afforded some relief by being allowed a carpenter to assist in making the wooden frames, while the work of making the moulds for less important paper, such as 'Loan Receipts' was given to Mary Smith, the former mould-maker, who had retired on Brewer's appointment, and who in 1805 was granted an annual allowance in consideration of her forty-one years' service in that capacity. Increased requirements of paper seemed to present no difficulties to Portal & Bridges,[1] who responded at all times to the repeated demands for more paper that were constantly made upon them. After the paper had arrived at the Bank, it was strictly controlled until it reached the process of damping when it was not possible to count it, but a balance of all paper was taken once a week in order to reach an agreement with the amount released, and a stock-taking of bank-notes and paper was carried out periodically by the cashiers who maintained an overall control of security.

The engraved plates had at first been locked in the Bank's Treasury each night, but the increased number in use soon made this procedure impracticable. More than fifty plates were kept in readiness from day to day, in order to print any of the fifteen[2] denominations that might be required, and it was arranged, therefore, that they should remain in the printing office at night, locked in an iron chest under the dual control of Terry and a clerk of the printing office. New plates were constantly required, and as each plate was completed a proof on 'common paper' was submitted to the Chief Cashier for his approval before the plate was taken into use. The output had now

---

[1] Joseph Portal, who had taken William Bridges into partnership, had died in 1793 and had been succeeded by his son John Portal.

[2] £1, £2, £5, £10, £15, £20, £25, £30, £40, £50, £100, £200, £300, £500 and £1000. The notes for £60, £70, £80, £90 and £400, which had never circulated to any great extent, had been discontinued.

risen to 30,000 notes per day, and six additional engravers, with whom the staff had been augmented, were kept continually at work on engraving new plates and repairing those which had become partially worn. Terry and his assistants were busy too, not only with the supervision of the whole of the work, but also with a new task that now fell to them, namely, examining, testing and reporting upon the numerous devices for the prevention of forgery that were being submitted to the Bank in increasing numbers. Inimitability was the keynote of the test, and in order to demonstrate, by making copies, the lack of that quality in the specimens submitted to them, it was necessary for them to execute a great deal of intricate engraving, which would be of no further use when it had served its single purpose.

During the whole of this time, Terry had been acquiring additional presses and asking for more space in which to use them, but in 1805 the position became serious. Terry reported that there were twenty-four presses in constant use and an equivalent number of pressmen, producing some 200 reams per week; that he had a total staff of fifty-one men, and that he required three more presses and two more engravers. Further, the present accommodation was inadequate, and the restricted quarters were causing illness among his men,[1] with consequent loss of output. He suggested that the only remedy was to allow some of the work to be done outside the Bank, for the permanent quarters for the printing department, which had been planned as far back as 1790, were still a thing of the future. The property upon which the north-west corner of the Bank was to be erected had been gradually acquired; Princes

[1] The copper plates were heated by charcoal, the fumes of which would, in a restricted space, aggravate the physical strain that a day's work on a hand press entailed.

Street had been straightened,[1] and Sir John Soane's curtain wall was in the course of erection. But the promised quarters had not been built and the need of the printing department was urgent. Arrangements were made to extend the accommodation then in use, and to allow less important work, such as bank-note lists and cheques, to be printed outside the Bank, at Terry's house. By the adoption of these expedients, the printers were able to fulfil their task for another three years, but, in March 1808, it was reported that the new premises were nearly completed, and it is probable that, later in that year, they were taken into use.[2]

As time went on, it became more and more evident that so large a part of the Bank's business should no longer be dependent upon a private firm, and in March 1808 it was decided 'that the Business of Printing Bank Notes be taken into the Hands of the Bank, and to be done within the Walls of the Bank by a Printer of their own, to be sworn in the Court of Directors as the rest of the Officers and Servants of the Bank are'. A month later, Terry was appointed copper-plate printer to the Bank at a salary of £1000 per annum, in consideration of his relinquishing his private business and 'of his having given up very considerable emoluments, which he derived from the Old System'. In order to avoid any misunderstanding in the mind of a potential successor, it was added that 'the Salary not to be drawn into a precedent for any future printer'.

---

[1] Princes Street, until powers were obtained in 1800 to straighten it, turned sharply to the right at a point near the present-day Princes Street entrance to the Bank, and then half-left in a north-easterly direction, to emerge into Lothbury immediately opposite St Margaret's Church.

[2] The same premises were occupied by the printing department, with expansion from time to time, until the move to Old Street (1917-20).

At the same time, a 'Storekeeper[1] of Bank Note Paper' was appointed, with responsibility for the custody of bank-note moulds and paper.

The steadily increasing demand for notes continued to present a problem, and, with a view to expediting output, the Bank had in 1807 considered a plan for printing the notes four on a sheet, instead of two as heretofore.[2] The moulds and the paper were made accordingly and with the help and advice of Robert Kirkwood, the bank-note printer of Edinburgh, some of the Bank's presses were adapted to print the larger sheet. Like many other labour-saving projects, however, this plan had its repercussions, and in December 1809 the Bank had to consider a petition from the pressmen in regard to their pay. It appeared that Terry paid 16s. 8d. per ream for work on the new presses (printing four notes at a time), and only 6s. 6d. per ream for work on the old ones. Terry admitted to the committee concerned that the new rate was too high, but that it had been granted in order to appease the pressmen, who had threatened to strike. The committee were of the opinion that Terry had 'acted extremely wrong', but they deferred the settlement of the printers' grievance. The matter continued to be deferred at subsequent meetings of the committee, extending into the following year, but there is no record of a settlement having been reached.

In the same year, Terry retired for reasons of ill health. In June 1810, J. H. Harper, his assistant, was appointed superintendent of the printing and engraving offices, and

[1] A storekeeper in charge of stores such as writing paper, pens, ink and sealing wax had been appointed in 1792.

[2] The original plan was to print the whole of the notes in this manner, but although the notes for £1 and £2 and some of £5, £10 and £100 were so printed, it would appear from existing examples that the denominations in less frequent demand were still printed two on a sheet.

the storekeeper appointed two years previously was furnished with a staff of six clerks to form the 'Storekeeper's Office for Bank Note Paper'. The printing department had found itself, and had started upon a course which has led, throughout the years, to the development of the vast organisation that it is today.

CHAPTER IV

NOTES FOR £1 AND £2 AND THE
INIMITABLE NOTE INQUIRY

THE RESTRICTION of cash payments was announced on 27 February 1797, and the Court of Directors, with a view to providing the country with small currency, immediately decided to issue notes for £1 and £2.[1] It was plain that the cashiers who normally signed the bank-notes would be unable to cope with the increase that was envisaged—actually, 700,000 notes were issued in the month of March 1797, whereas 100,000 had sufficed for the preceding month—and consequently six clerks of lower rank were appointed to sign the new notes. It was to the printers, however, that there fell the task of providing the required notes, and it is to their credit that they fulfilled this task within the space of three days, the notes being ready for issue on 2 March. But this speedy result was attained only by re-engraving upon old and worn-out plates, which had already served their turn for notes of higher denominations, and consequently the hastily executed work on such a foundation was below the usual standard. The notes were the same size ($4\frac{1}{2}$ inches by 8 inches) and on the same plan as those of higher sums, but as soon as new plates could be engraved, a process which was completed in 1798, a change was made. The paper remained the same size but the printed portion was reduced to $3\frac{1}{4}$ inches by 6 inches and enclosed by a thin

[1] The Act of 1777, by which the issue of notes for less than £5 had been prohibited, was speedily amended.

engraved line. The resultant margin was left blank, except that the words ONE or TWO, as the case might be were printed upon it in roman capitals at the head of the paper.

The new notes performed adequately their function of providing a highly necessary currency, but the issue was followed by an unforeseen and unfortunate circumstance —a vast increase in the number of forged notes. One of the causes of this increase was the fact that, while hitherto the bank-notes for higher sums had circulated among people of substance who were accustomed to handling security documents, the new notes were in daily use among a widely different class, who had no such experience, and who might even be illiterate. Here, then, was an opportunity for the forgers, who lost no time in taking advantage of the ignorance of their fellows.

Forgery, as we have seen, had always been a matter of concern to the Bank, and constant attention had been paid to the means of combating it. Nevertheless, the number of forged notes had, except for sporadic outbreaks,[1] never been great, and when, at the close of the year 1797, it was seen that during the year there had been a considerable increase in the number of forgeries, immediate steps were taken to discover a means of countering the menace. Consultations took place with 'men of science and eminent artists', and the Bank let it be known that they would be open to consider any suggestions for the improvement of the notes, which would render them less likely to be forged. No specific reward was offered, but it was made clear that the author of any suggestion which it was decided to adopt would be liberally recompensed.[2] The result was a spate of suggestions from all over the country. Forty years

[1] Notably from 1780 to 1785, when the extensive forgeries of Charles Price, alias 'Old Patch', had given the Bank cause for anxiety.

[2] In some instances 'of superior promise', financial aid was given to the proposers, in order that they might put their plans into effect.

later, when this subject again came up for discussion, the situation was summed up by the Governor of the period in the words 'the multiplicity of proposed schemes, the absurdity of many and the inefficiency of others had tended to embarrass and protract the subject rather than add any useful information or facilities in respect to it', and truth to tell the statement was a fair description of many of the suggestions—there were in all nearly four hundred of them—that flowed into the Bank from all sides.

A number of these suggestions came from people who, before they would divulge their secrets, required to know the amount of the reward that they would receive. One went so far as to stipulate for a payment of £2000 in advance, and also that he should be made a director of the Bank! The comments of the Court of Directors on this demand are not recorded, but in a subsequent report it was stated that generally 'the plans of those persons, who stipulated in the first instance for remuneration, proved, of all others, the least deserving of notice'. Some of the proposals would have been most useful if they had not, at the same time, been entirely impracticable. It does not, for example, call for much imagination to discern the impracticability of a suggestion that the number and date of each note should be shown in the watermark! Quite a number of the applicants for consideration proposed devices which would facilitate the discovery of a forged note at its examination after it had returned to the Bank, having lost sight of the Bank's object, namely the prevention of forgery. Several suggestions were based on the introduction into the design of a fortuitous impression to be produced by a piece of broken steel, or of an engraving upon glass, which, having been subsequently broken, would defy imitation of the haphazard cracks so produced. The authors of such suggestions, as well as those who suggested a highly complicated or involved design, ignored the fact that an out-of-the-way or unusual design, as well as one full of detail, is easier to imitate well enough to deceive all but the expert eye than is a simple pattern that can be easily grasped and kept in mind by the public, whose protection in this matter was the foremost consideration. The protection envisaged by the Bank, however, was to be brought about by means of an improved note, but some of the suggestions that were received, without making any contribution in this respect, proposed plans for the protection of the public by such means as the stationing of inspectors in the principal streets of the Metropolis, in order apparently that their opinion might be obtained before a proffered note was accepted, while others suggested that a number of clerks, furnished with large quantities of silver coin, should be similarly stationed, in order presumably that notes might be quickly cashed and the anxiety of the holder appeased.

But it will be more useful if we turn to some of the practical schemes that were received. The dictum that 'what one man can do, another can imitate' was prominently in the minds of the committee concerned, but ease or difficulty of imitation was considered of importance, and was the usual test employed. The first recorded instance of a practical proposal was that of Alexander Tilloch, an engraver of Carey Street, who approached the Bank as early as May 1797, and informed them that he had an engraving to show them which he declared to be inimitable. He was, accordingly, invited to attend at the Bank with examples of his work, and on 9 May he appeared, accompanied by 'Mr Bartolozzi and Mr Heath',[1] who gave their enthusias-

[1] Francesco Bartolozzi, the fashionable engraver of the period. James Heath, historical engraver to George III. Tilloch was supported also by John Landseer, a prominent engraver, who was later to be the father of Sir Edwin Landseer, but he did not appear in person.

tic support to his claim. Then followed the procedure which became, in subsequent instances, almost a routine. Garnet Terry, the Bank's engraver, was given a proof of Tilloch's plate, and in due course produced a copy, which it was considered, although it was plate-printed while Tilloch's engraving was in relief for surface-printing, would effectively deceive the public. Tilloch was informed accordingly, and retired from the contest, although he was to reappear some twenty years later in controversial circumstances. Another proposal was received in the same year from Anthony Bessemer, who, although his reputation has been overshadowed by that of his more famous son Sir Henry, was possessed of considerable inventive ability; he had only just escaped from Paris, where, before the revolution, he had been employed in the French Mint. Unfortunately, there is no record of the nature of his plan, except for Terry's report that it was 'very liable to be imitated'. Among other early proposals was one from Jeremy Bentham, who, although he is chiefly remembered as the founder of the Utilitarian school of philosophy, was a man of the widest interests, as is instanced by this incursion into the field of bank-note production. His contribution recommended a combination of the arts, a principle which was included in many subsequent proposals, the idea being that, while one venal artist might be found the collusion of several would be unlikely. As a vignette, he recommended a finely engraved portrait, recognised nowadays, on account of the ease with which it may be remembered, to be one of the best means of ensuring security. The proposal was, however, not accepted, probably on account of the impracticability of reproducing as many identical copies of a finely engraved portrait as would suffice for the numerous copper plates that were required.

In 1800, the number of forged notes rose to 4000, but,

in that year, there was adopted a plan, which the Bank had
been considering for some time, and which did much to
stem the tide of forgeries. This scheme had its origin in
1798, when William Brewer, a watermark mould-maker of
Maidstone, who came of a family which had for long been
engaged in that work, approached the Bank with a plan for
making a change in the design of the watermark, which had
remained practically unaltered for more than a hundred
years. For the better appreciation of this plan it should be
mentioned that the wires, from which a paper-making
mould was constructed, were set parallel to one another
and ran in straight lines along the length of the mould. At
intervals of about one or two inches they were strengthened
by being sewn together with other wires, which crossed
the 'laid' wires at right angles, producing the well-known
effect to be seen when a piece of 'laid' paper is held to the
light.[1] Brewer's plan was to make a mould in which both
'laid lines' and the lines that crossed them should be waved
instead of being straight. During the subsequent trials
and experiments, a further protective device was introduced by including in the design of the watermark the denomination of the notes, and in 1800 it was decided to
adopt both of these improvements for the notes of £1 and
£2, the denominations of which were to be shown in bold
roman capitals across the middle of the notes. In the same
year, Brewer was appointed mould-maker to the Bank, and
Portal & Bridges proceeded with the manufacture of the
new paper. At the same time, it was decided to abandon
the practice adopted in 1798 whereby the size of the
printed portion of the notes had been reduced, and the
engraving again occupied the whole of the paper. The

[1] 'Wove' paper, which was invented at about the middle of the
eighteenth century, was made upon a mould of pierced metal or plain
wire gauze, and showed, therefore, no lines.

printed denominations at the head of the notes were retained, but that of the £1 notes was now in italic capitals,[1]
and that of the £2 notes in gothic type. A further change
was made in the notes for £2 by setting the sum piece at an
angle of approximately 20 degrees to the horizontal alignment of the remainder of the text. This change would
appear to have been designed in order to help the illiterate,
but the resultant appearance was far from pleasing, and the
customary alignment was restored in 1810. Production of
the new notes was put in hand at once, and early in 1801
an Act of Parliament was passed, by which the manufacture of any paper, the watermark of which embodied
waved lines, was prohibited.[2] In July 1801, a notice was
inserted in the *London Gazette* to notify the public of the
changes, and to inform them that on the 31st of that
month, the new notes would be issued.

The public were encouraged to exchange the notes in
their possession for others of the new pattern, but the old
notes which continued in circulation were still extensively
forged. The total for 1801 amounted to nearly 8000, and,
in order to cope with the consequent increase in the number of suggestions that were submitted to the Bank, it was
decided, in 1802, to appoint a 'Committee to examine
plans for the Improvement of Bank Notes'. Among the
first of these plans was one from Thomas Bewick, who
submitted a wood engraving, which art he was engaged in
raising to a new and previously unheard-of height, but
Terry was able to produce a creditable imitation by copper-
plate engraving, and the plan was rejected. Other plans
recommended embossing and die-stamping, but neither

[1] The use of roman capitals was resumed in 1810.
[2] The prohibition still exists, and to this day no paper maker is
allowed to use a watermark embodying a waved line without having
first obtained the Bank's permission.

E

was considered suitable, on account of the thinness of the paper. A note printed by letterpress that should be peculiar to the Bank and prohibited to all others, a proposal which was repeated on several subsequent occasions, was regarded as being easily imitated. Plate-printing upon silk instead of paper was not satisfactory but a proposal that silk threads should be embodied in the substance of the paper was strangely prophetic, for many years later this practice was adopted by several foreign countries as a security measure. M. Guillot, the manufacturer of the paper used for the notes of the Banque de France, submitted specimens of his product, but suggestions in regard to the improvement of paper were inappropriate at a time when the new paper embodying Brewer's innovations was proving highly successful. The number of forged notes, which had been steadily increasing during the previous five years, fell in 1802 to 5000 ,and the committee, in a report of March 1803, declared that they were satisfied with the paper then in use. The committee also commented upon the various plans that they had examined, and declared that, in spite of the ingenuity of many, which would have made difficult the production of a perfect imitation capable of deceiving an expert, it was found to be a 'comparatively easy and practicable matter to produce a Copy as would impose upon the public'. In conclusion, it was stated that they could not recommend any alteration in the notes as they then were, and the committee was accordingly dissolved, while the Committee of Treasury resumed the consideration of the plans that were submitted.

In 1805 a minor change was made in the form of the £2 note. It was not an anti-forgery device, but merely a vertical line down the middle of the note, to serve as a guide when notes were cut in half for the purpose of ensuring safety in the post. It was proposed to add this line to the notes for £1, but the intention was never carried out, and thus for five years, until 1810 when it was discontinued, the vertical line served as an additional means of identification to the illiterate. The printing of numbers and dates, introduced in 1809, was again not intended as a security measure, but incidentally it had that effect. The fact that the numbers were overprinted upon the text increased considerably the difficulty of altering the numbers of, say, a stolen note the numbers of which were known. Moreover, the counterfeiter would, in many instances, not trouble to employ a second process, and would engrave the number and date on his plate with the remainder of the text. Thus, all the notes printed from such a plate bore the same number and date, a fact which provided a useful means of identification.

The effect of the improved paper continued to make itself felt. In 1803, the number of forged notes fell to 3000, a figure which was maintained, with slight variations, for several years, and it seemed as if the tide had turned. It was appreciated, nevertheless, that the figure was altogether too high, and constant attention was given to the proposals that continued to be received. It seemed, however, as if all the possibilities had been exhausted, for the plans that were now submitted bore a striking resemblance to those which had been received in the past, and the reply that their 'suggestion had been anticipated and already considered' had frequently to be made to the authors of such plans. The subject of paper loomed large among the suggestions that were received and coloured or particoloured paper was frequently recommended. It was considered, however, that the constant variation that would arise from the impossibility of maintaining identity of colour was likely to be a danger rather than a protection. The proposal, repeatedly made, that the design of the note should contain a 'fine' engraving by a master-hand was negatived by the fact that the master-hand itself—for no other would do—could never cope with the continual engraving of reproductions of the original design, which would be necessary for the large number of plates that were required.

As time went on, however, it seemed that this difficulty might be solved. As we have seen, Jacob Perkins had recently revived the art of engraving upon steel, and the large number of impressions that might be obtained from an engraved steel plate, and the even greater number that it would produce after it had been hardened[1] brought the possibility of the master-hand into the picture. This matter came to a head in 1811 when the Bank was approached by J. C. Dyer, who, it will be remembered, had in the previous year patented Jacob Perkins's 'check plate' in this country, and who now submitted specimens of the New England notes which had been produced by that process. The usual routine was followed and J. H. Harper, who had succeeded Garnet Terry as superintendent of printing and engraving, produced an effective copy from a copper plate. But the Bank's interest in steel engraving had been aroused, and in the following year Dyer was asked to supply steel plates, upon which the Bank's engravers could experiment, and to provide a press[2] upon which to print from them. Unfortunately, the experiment was not a success. In May 1813, Harper reported that the engraving took four times as long as that of a copper plate, and that the attempts to harden the plates had been singu-

[1] Modern methods of hardening steel were not then invented; hardening was effected by heating the metal in a closed container packed with leather charcoal.

[2] The steel plates were very much thicker than the copper plates in use, and were consequently beyond the scope of the ordinary press.

larly unsuccessful, one half of them having broken during the process. He complained, too, of spots and blemishes that appeared on the unengraved portion of the plate, due to the oxidisation of the steel, and also that he had succeeded in producing only 35,000 impressions from one plate. He went on, moreover, to make the surprising statement that, while normally a copper plate would produce 15,000 impressions, by dint of what he euphemistically described as 'retouching and repair'—a process which must have amounted in effect to complete re-engraving—150,000 to 200,000 impressions would be produced from each copper plate! In these circumstances, identity of the notes could hardly be expected, and it is a matter for regret that experiments with steel were not pursued to a successful issue. Some of the fault may be due to the fact that they were carried out under the supervision of the 'patentee of the American Bank Notes', that is to say, J. C. Dyer, who, although an expert in many branches of mechanics, was not an engraver.

In 1812, the Bank's characteristic sum piece was protected by an Act of Parliament, by which the use of white letters on a black ground was prohibited to all printers except those authorised by the Bank, and in order to comply with the Act, J. H. Harper was in that year so authorised. The Act did not come into force until the end of the following year, in order that a number of country banks, whose notes embodied this feature, might change their designs and arrange for the engraving of new plates. But although the law-abiding were inconvenienced by the Act, it left the forgers unmoved, and the lull in the number of forged notes that had set in in 1803 showed signs of being followed by the proverbial storm. In 1811, the number of forged notes had risen to 9000, and in the following year, it reached 18,000. This figure, after another lull, rose in 1816, possibly on account of the increase of crime that is to be expected in a post-war period, to 25,000, and in 1817 it reached the alarming figure of 31,000. Now the interest that the public had taken in furthering the anti-forgery campaign had been due not only to a desire for their own protection, but also to a strong feeling of sympathy for the unfortunate people who were, with increasing frequency, convicted and hanged, for unfortunate they were in that in most instances they were poor and ignorant folk, who had been persuaded to engage in the crime of 'uttering' by the actual forgers, in whose place they suffered. The forgers themselves, who were rarely brought to justice, were few in number, for it was estimated from the expert examination which was given to all forged notes, that the alarming number of forgeries in circulation were produced from not more than ten plates, and that only six of these were then in use. In 1817, the erstwhile sympathy of the public was changed to indignation when it was known that, since the beginning of the restriction of cash payments, no less than 313 persons had been sentenced to death for passing forged notes, and a marked increase took place in the stream of suggestions that daily flowed into the Bank. It was decided, accordingly, to revive the committee which had been dissolved in 1803, and in December 1817 a 'Committee to examine plans for the Improvement of Bank Notes, and for the Prevention of Forgery' was appointed.

One of the first items for the consideration of this committee was a letter from Augustus Applegarth, a prominent printer of considerable inventive ability. He proposed surface-printing in several colours from blocks to be produced by stereotype, in accordance with an invention that he was then perfecting,[1] from an original relief cut in

[1] The 'flong', or papier mâché matrix, which is now in general use for casting stereotype plates, was not then invented and plates were

wood or metal. Applegarth drew attention to the fact that
there were very few engravers in relief who would be able
to imitate the work of 'a first rate Artist in that line', and
that a preponderance of white designs upon black would
render difficult an attempt to imitate them by a copper-
plate engraver. The committee were attracted by the suggestion and, after some negotiation, the sum of £1200 was
advanced to Applegarth, in order that he and his partner,
Edward Cowper, who was the inventor of several ingenious devices and also a skilful engineer, might go forward
with their plan. The two partners accordingly returned to
Croydon, where, with a view to preserving the secrecy of
their process, they had set up their works, and proceeded
with the production of proofs for the consideration of the
committee, who continued to examine the many other
plans that were submitted to them. One of these was from
J. T. B. Beaumont, who recommended a finely engraved
vignette occupying one third of the whole design, with a
die-stamped border. As we know, there were reasons why
neither of these methods could be used, and Beaumont
was informed accordingly. He was, however, not satisfied
and placed his scheme before the Society for the Encouragement of Arts, Manufactures and Commerce, of
which he was a member.

This society, which had been founded in 1754, was, as
its name implied, engaged in the encouragement of the
Polite Arts, Agriculture, Chemistry, Manufactures, Mechanics, etc., and had done work of great value in the advancement of its objects by the encouragement of new
ideas and inventions and by the promotion of a number of

cast either from matrices of plaster of Paris, or by the method invented by William Ged in the early eighteenth century, in which the
matrix was made by immersing the original forme of type, or relief
block, in molten metal at the moment when it was about to solidify.
Applegarth's invention was a variation of this method.

exhibitions.[1] The society decided that it would be within their scope to endeavour to find a means 'not for totally preventing the forgery of Bank Notes (for that is obviously impossible) but for increasing the difficulty of imitation', and appointed a committee to hear evidence and to consider suggestions which might be of value in that connection. While this committee proceeded with its deliberations, a more official body was set up when in April 1818 the Government, in response to persistent public agitation, appointed a Royal Commission 'for enquiring into the mode of preventing the Forgery of Bank Notes'. The first step of the Royal Commission, after the members had established themselves at a house in Soho Square, was to ask for a full account of all that the Bank had already done in the matter. The Bank responded with a long and detailed report of the action that had been taken, with much of which we are acquainted. It would appear that but few plans were submitted directly to the Royal Commission, who were chiefly occupied in reviewing the more useful of the plans received by the Bank, which were submitted to the Commission after the Bank's committee had given them consideration.

During the year 1818, the Bank's committee was kept fully occupied by the suggestions that flowed in from a public still indignant at the steadily increasing number of executions. One correspondent suggested that the cashiers and clerks who signed the notes should be made to write more legibly, and another that the written signature was by no means necessary, so that it might well be printed to-

[1] In later years, as the Royal Society of Arts—it received its Royal Charter in 1847—it was the originator of the Great Exhibition of 1851 as well as of many subsequent exhibitions, and continues today, by means of bursaries and awards, to exercise its original function of encouraging art and industry.

gether with the rest of the note. This suggestion was given consideration and steps were taken to obtain the necessary authority, with the result that, two years later, an Act of Parliament was passed, by which authority was given for the signatures to be printed instead of being written by hand. But for some reason which is not now apparent, this authority was never exercised, and the notes continued to be signed by hand. Two other suggestions harked back to protective measures long since tried and abandoned —an indented note, and a note of which a portion of the paper should be marbled—while another was strangely prophetic in proposing a lithographed design on the reverse. Rudolph Ackerman, the print-seller in the Strand, was also prophetic in recommending a process which was much used in later years, namely, machine engraving transferred to stone for reproduction by lithography, of which art Ackerman was an enthusiastic supporter. He had used it extensively in the production of his popular *Repository* and had published a translation of Senefelder's *Der Steindruck*,[1] under the name of *A Complete Course of Lithography*. But the Bank were definitely opposed to lithography, which was described in a subsequent report to the Royal Commission in the words 'a discovery as applied to the subject of Forgery, infinitely more to be dreaded than encouraged'. Apart from lithographic reproduction, actual machine engraving, which was then coming into its own, was frequently recommended, notably by

[1] The art of lithography, which was discovered by Alois Senefelder in 1798, differs from both relief and plate printing in that the impression is produced from a perfectly flat stone. The design to be reproduced is drawn on or transferred to a slab of absorbent stone in greasy chalk or ink. After further treatment the stone is then wetted, so that the ink, subsequently applied, is repelled by the wet stone, but adheres to the greasy design which is then reproduced on paper under pressure.

J. L. Bradbury—an early mention, in that connection, of a name, which now has a world-wide association with engraving—but machine engraving, as we have seen in the instance of the New England notes, had been successfully imitated by the Bank's engravers.

Anthony Bessemer, who now made a second appearance, had, while rebuilding the fortune lost by him during the French Revolution, entered into an alliance with Henry Caslon, and had set up a typefoundry in Hertfordshire. He submitted a reproduction of letterpress, engraved in recess, to be printed in register, on both sides of the paper, and John Landseer, who had withdrawn his support of Alexander Tilloch, proposed a letterpress note with a die-stamped border, but, as we know, both of these projects were considered impracticable on account of the thinness of the paper. Tilloch himself then made a reappearance, and submitted his original engraving with a coloured design on the reverse. Terry's imitation, engraved twenty-one years before, was produced to him, whereupon Tilloch criticised it in the plainest terms, and pointed out several details in which it differed widely from his engraving. Fortunately, the Bank had retained an impression from Tilloch's original plate, which showed that the plate which he now produced had been altered in several particulars, thereby producing the very differences that he had pointed out! 'The Committee could not forbear express their surprise and displeasure at the alteration'; but the matter did not end there, and in their Report to the Court of Directors the committee commented, not only upon the episode of the alteration, but also upon Tilloch's subsequent action in publishing in the *Star* newspaper, of which he was the editor and chief proprietor, 'whole columns of calumnies and misimputations worded in language the most inflammatory', and went on to say that 'there can be no question that to this source may be traced much of the prejudice which has taken deep root in the public mind'.

A further effort for recognition was made by J. C. Dyer, Jacob Perkins's representative, who produced once more the New England notes that Terry had successfully imitated seven years before, but the record of this fact, as well perhaps as the recollection of Dyer's having supervised the unfortunate attempt to engrave on steel, did not encourage the committee to reconsider his plan. But a few months later, the Bank was approached by Jacob Perkins himself, who had come over from America, together with Gideon Fairman and Asa Spencer,[1] in order to take part in the anti-forgery campaign. He submitted specimens of new and improved notes, which had been produced by means of his plate transfer press,[2] and which were specially designed to illustrate the scope of his invention. In the one here reproduced (Plate VII), for example, both of the vignettes, the stipple-engraved[3] portrait of the Prince Regent and the line engraving of Britannia, are repeated in order to show the complete identity of each pair, while the side panels are made up of a comprehensive variety of machine engraving, including white line work.[4] The micro-tint, consisting of the words 'one pound' repeated nearly two thousand times, of which the central panels are composed, and which it would be practically impossible to engrave by hand, was produced by designing, in a reasonable size, only a small part of the whole, reducing it

[1] See p. 35 above.
[2] See p. 35 above.
[3] Stippling is sometimes used in conjunction with line engraving, but in true stipple engraving there are no lines; the engraver produces the effect of high lights, deep shades and middle tones solely by the use of dots of varying sizes and at varying distances apart.
[4] By the introduction of an additional step in the process of transferring, lines which would have appeared black if printed from the original engraving are reproduced as white on a black ground.

by means of the pantograph,[1] etching, and finally rolling in by the transfer press. The submission of these specimens to the Bank and to the Royal Commission—for a separate approach was made to that body—was accompanied by a pamphlet, written by J. C. Dyer. In this pamphlet he described the advantages of the process, referred to as 'siderography', and expressed his fear that it might be prejudiced because it had been 'suggested by a foreigner'. In this connection, he stressed the fact that, as Perkins's system was a going concern which had been in operation for some years in America, the Bank would be able to install and use it at once, instead of waiting for what he described as the 'doubtful issue' of the English experiments then proceeding. This implication that Applegarth and Cowper were taking rather a long time over the development of their plan, was followed by a more direct criticism regarding their insistence upon secrecy. There was, he explained, no secret about Perkins's method, which, he declared, could be shown and even explained to a forger, in the sure knowledge that he would be quite unable to put it into practice.

In spite of Dyer's enthusiastic advocacy, the Bank allowed the usual routine to proceed, and after Harper had imitated some of the most difficult parts of the intricate machine engraving and the committee had given the matter prolonged consideration, they reported that they were unable 'to avail themselves of the talents of that most able and ingenious Artist'. Disappointed, but undismayed, Perkins proceeded to perfect his plate transfer press, which he patented in the following year, and set up in business

[1] The pantograph is an instrument in which a point known as the 'tracer', is moved over the lines of an original design and is linked to another point, which repeats each of its movements. By this process, a design may be simply copied or, by an appropriate adjustment of the linkage, either enlarged or reduced.

VII. Specimen note submitted by Jacob Perkins in 1818.
Actual size 4¾ in. × 8 in.

with Gideon Fairman as bank-note printers. Asa Spencer had by this time returned to America, and the new firm took into partnership Charles Heath, a son of James Heath.[1] The Bank were to hear a great deal more of Charles Heath, for he persisted for some years, even after the end of the restriction of cash payments, in trying to arouse the Bank's interest in the work of his firm. There were, however, few competitors still in the arena, and Applegarth and Cowper, who now produced specimens in colour that received the full approval of the committee, seemed to be ensured of success. Their latest specimens were approved by the Court of Directors, who decided, on 4 February 1819, to submit them to the Royal Commission. It was understood that the Commission approved; the Committee to Examine Plans was accordingly dissolved, and the Committee of Treasury, reinforced for the purpose, continued to perform that task.

In the same year, the Royal Commission issued a report, in which they stated that they had examined 108 projects and the methods followed in order to test them, as well as 70 varieties of paper. They also recapitulated much that we already know of the plans submitted to the Bank, and stated that they had sought information from the paper currency of other countries, more particularly that of America. They recommended that pecuniary rewards should be made for the apprehension and conviction of persons actually engaged in forgery, an appreciation of the fact that the actual perpetrators of the crime were seldom brought to justice. The commission expressed surprise at the fact that the public were so easily deceived by poor imitations, and suggested that carelessness in this regard would lessen the good effect that would otherwise be derived from the employment of superior skill and workman-

[1] See p. 50 n.

ship in the production of the notes. With a view to countering this tendency, it was urged upon the public that all notes coming into their possession should be subjected to a cautious examination of the whole of each note. In conclusion, the commission suggested that safety should be sought in a 'combination of excellence beyond the reach of the copper-plate printer', a quality which was, in the opinion of the commission, embodied in the plan 'now being supported by the Bank'. The plan referred to, although not mentioned by name, was that of Applegarth and Cowper.

It was in 1819, too, that the Society of Arts issued their report, which, although it did not carry the weight of that of the Royal Commission, was an infinitely more lively production and made a valuable contribution to the inquiry. Generally speaking, the society advocated a combination of the arts, a finely engraved vignette and machine engraving, while once again the copper-plate engraver figured as the villain of the piece. It was stated that there were no less than 10,000 copper-plate engravers in the country capable of copying a Bank of England note; that nine-tenths of them were needy and that many were in distressed circumstances. Hence the recommendation in favour of a combination of the Arts, which would necessitate the employment of a number of persons of different crafts, and of machine engraving, involving the use of heavy and expensive plant, which would be beyond the scope of the obscure forger, working in a back room and printing in a cellar. The security obtained by the employment of a multiplicity of craftsmen was particularly emphasised by T. C. Hansard, the son of Luke Hansard, printer to the House of Commons, whose name lives today in connection with the records of the House. Hansard, who submitted a typographical note, stated that no less than twenty different arts and crafts were employed in the processes of engraving, die-sinking, typefounding, stereo-typing and printing, necessary for the production of his note, and that no one forger could possibly possess the ability to perform them all. The outstanding feature of Hansard's note was the use of letterpress in diamond type, the smallest type but one normally in use. Henry Caslon, who had cast this particular fount, stated that the punches[1] were cut by Anthony Bessemer, who thus made yet another entry into the arena, and that there were not more than four or five artists in the country, capable of executing similar work. As a further protection, it was proposed that it should be made unlawful for any person to make or to handle diamond type unless authorised by the Bank.

Machine engraving had many advocates. It had been taken up with enthusiasm by a number of engravers, and specimens printed from plates engraved by means of the ruling machine and the rose engine[2] loomed large among the plans considered by the committee of the Society of Arts. The fact arose that the notes of country banks were forged but infrequently, and Harry Ashby as well as Richard Silvester, whom we have noted as prominent bank-note printers of the period, stated in evidence that the absence of forgery was due to the superior engraving of their vignettes. It does not seem, however, to have been considered that, as the issues of the country banks were comparatively small, the difficulty in regard to the frequent re-engraving of a fine vignette did not arise.

One of the most attractive and well executed of the engravings submitted to the society was that of T. F. Ranson, who had previously approached the Bank directly. It would seem, however, that his powers of expression did

1 The first step in the manufacture of type is the cutting, in relief, of a steel punch. This punch is then 'struck' into copper to form a matrix from which the type is then cast. (This note is printed in diamond type.)

2 See p. 34 above.

not equal his skill as an engraver, for it is recorded that the Bank found his communication to be 'incoherent'. But Ranson had even less pleasant recollections of his relations with the Bank, for early in 1818 he had been involved in a dispute with one of the Bank's investigators[1] in regard to a forged note, which he had received in the ordinary course of business, and which had been impounded.[2] Ranson regained possession of the note by means of a ruse, and refused to surrender it. He was, accordingly, arrested and committed to Coldbath Fields Prison, where he was confined only for four days before he was released on bail. As, however, the Bank decided not to offer evidence, Ranson was discharged, whereupon he brought an action against the investigator, who had been the cause of his 'false and malicious imprisonment' and was later awarded £100 damages.[3] Ranson subsequently published an interesting memento of his incarceration, in the form of an engraving, in which he depicted himself in prison, gazing at the barred windows of his cell. An appropriate legend relates the circumstances of his imprisonment, and concludes with a note to the effect that the work is 'dedicated without permission to the Governor and Company of the Threadneedle Street Paper Establishment'. Ranson's imprisonment had taken place during the month of February 1818,

---

[1] Notes, when presented at the Bank, were examined by 'inspectors', and any found to be forgeries were passed to 'investigators', who carried out the function that their name implies.

[2] At this time, all forged notes that were discovered were retained by the Bank. Criticism of this practice had been voiced before the Committee of the Society of Arts, for, it was said, 'it is only by comparing them together that the public can learn to discover the superior execution of the genuine notes over the forged ones'. A few months later in June 1818 the practice was discontinued, and, for some time after that date, forged notes, after having been indelibly stamped with the word 'Forged', were returned to the holders.

[3] W. Marston Acres, *The Bank of England from Within*, p. 347.

VIII. Design for a note submitted by T. F. Ranson in 1818.
Actual size $4\frac{3}{4}$ in. × $7\frac{1}{2}$ in.

and in April of the same year he submitted his note to the Society of Arts. With commendable discretion, he made no mention of the Bank in his letter, but stated that he had been induced to offer his plan 'from a wish that . . . . the sacrifice of human life may be checked, and the laborious tradesman may be no longer obliged to bear the heavy losses to which he is now subjected'. The note, which was a delightful production (Plate VIII), was the work of no less than five hands. P. Archer and E. Turrell executed the machine engraving in which process they were experts, and Mark Lambert the text. Ranson's work was confined to the engraving of the vignette from a picture painted for this purpose by J. Thurston.

The report of the Society of Arts was issued early in 1819, but there is no record of any reaction on the part of the Bank, who were by that time confident that they had found the solution of their difficulties in the work of Apple-garth and Cowper. Throughout that year, they submitted a succession of specimens in varying colours, which never failed to earn approval, and in October 1819 arrangements were made for their work to be carried on within the Bank. In the previous year, the Governor had been authorised to advance to Applegarth and Cowper sums of money, not exceeding £5000 on each occasion. Several such advances were made, while further expense was incurred in the pro-vision of premises for the accommodation of a steam engine, by which their machinery was to be driven, and quarters, in which the work might be carried out in secret. This secrecy—for nothing was known save that the notes were printed from stereotype plates—lent to the work of Applegarth and Cowper an air of mystery, which added in no small degree to the interest evoked by their productions. The main design was in black, interspersed with patterns in one or more colours, while the design of the back was a

F

reversed impression of that upon the front, and in register with it. The perfect register of the coloured portions, as well as that of the reversed impression on the back of the notes with the design on the front, led to much speculation as to the means whereby it was attained, but the secrecy no longer exists, and we now know exactly how it was done.

Their press, which, according to Cowper, printed 1200 notes per hour, was built on the principle of a cylinder machine for printing wallpaper, invented by him in 1816, and use was made of two further inventions of his, a method by which stereotype plates might be bent to fit the cylinders, and a device for inking by means of rollers. In later years, Cowper wrote to a friend of his, who had asked for information regarding the methods employed by him and his partner, and in this letter[1] Cowper enclosed a sketch of the press, from which may be seen the manner in which it worked. The drawing is only diagramatic and shows nothing of the mechanism, but the principle of the machine is made clear. The perfect register of the colours was achieved by the nice adjustment of the printing plates by means of fine-threaded screws and by the tension of the tapes which carried the paper from one cylinder to the next. The registration of the reversed design on the back of the notes was due, apart from the tapes, to the fact that the back was not, strictly speaking, printed at all, but 'set off', that is to say, the paper received the impression on the back, not from the stereotype plate itself, but from an impression, of which the ink was still wet, previously printed on a leather pad.[2] Thus it required two revolutions of the machine to print one sheet. The first was made with no paper in the machine, and the impressions were made

[1] Now in the Museum collections of the Bank of England.

[2] One of these pads, with the impression still upon it, remains to this day in the possession of St Luke's Printing Works.

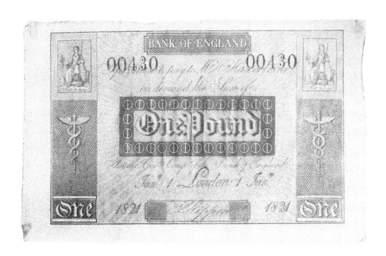

IX. The Applegarth and Cowper note.
Actual size 5 in. × 8 in.

upon the leather pads, one of which was fixed to each of the impression cylinders. At the next revolution, paper having been inserted, the front and the back of the note were both printed and set off simultaneously.

While Applegarth and Cowper were proceeding with their work, the Bank had to consider another scheme for printing in more than one colour, on this occasion from Sir William Congreve, who was in a curious position since he was a member of the Royal Commission and, at the same time, a participant in the arena. Sir William was a man of outstanding ingenuity, who was responsible for a number of inventions in different branches of science and industry. His colour-printing device consisted of a plate of hard metal, through which an open-work pattern was cut, and which was then filled with molten metal to form a second plate. The two plates were then separated, inked in different colours, reassembled and used for printing. The specimens submitted by Sir William were given due con-sideration, but by this time the Bank were firmly wedded to the colour-printing device of Applegarth and Cowper, and the plan was rejected.

Congreve, however, was never without several irons in the fire. The one to which he now turned was the improve-ment of paper, a subject upon which he had been experi-menting for some time, and he submitted a plan to the Bank which would require the collaboration of both mould-maker and paper-maker. Now the Bank had given pro-longed consideration to the subject of paper, and for some years past William Brewer, the mould-maker, had been a frequent visitor to the mill where Portal and Bridges had been carrying out experiments on behalf of the Bank, as well as a number on their own initiative. Perhaps on account of the constant travelling necessitated by these experiments —Laverstoke is nearly sixty miles from London—it was proposed that the Bank should erect their own paper mill in a locality, as John Rennie put it 'most convenient to the Establishment'. Rennie, who, although he is chiefly remembered as a civil engineer,[1] was also a mechanical engineer of distinction, had been called in to advise on the installation of steam power for driving the necessary machinery, since the place 'convenient to the Establishment' would probably not be provided with water-power, by means of which the mill at Laverstoke functioned. Rennie prepared plans and reported on the advantages of such a scheme, but the matter seems to have gone no further. Applegarth, in addition to his many other requirements, had made demands in regard to paper, which, he insisted, should be of special quality and texture, and Portal and Bridges were obliged to install additional plant in order to meet his needs. Then Brewer, whose services the Bank had agreed to lend, in order that he might put Sir William Congreve's plan into practice, again appeared at the paper-mill, and John Portal, who by this time was in sole direction of the mill—William Bridges had died in 1819—co-operated by providing labour and materials. The operation consisted of the production of Sir William's 'triple paper', of which the distinctive feature was a coloured watermark. Three separate sheets of extremely thin paper—one of them coloured, or parti-coloured by the use of stencils—were dipped and 'couched' one on another, with the coloured sheet in the middle, so that, after pressure, they dried as one sheet. Thus, the paper, which showed the watermark but faintly, would, on being held to the light, fully reveal the colour which was embedded between the outside layers. Many experiments were carried out on these lines, and finally a method was evolved

[1] He had only just completed the construction of his *chef d'oeuvre*, Waterloo Bridge.

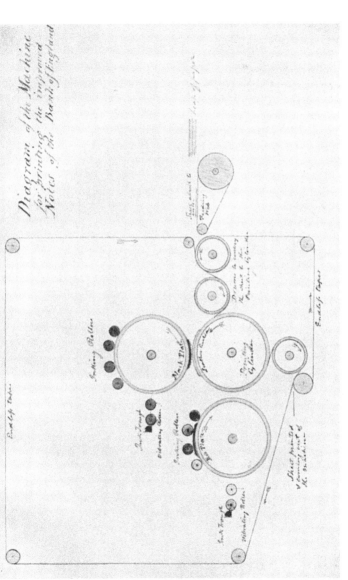

X. Applegarth and Cowper's press

whereby the required effect was produced by three dip-pings and one 'couching'.[1] The resultant specimens were submitted to the Bank, but, as we know, they were opposed to the use of colour in paper, on account of the difficulty of maintaining its identity. The situation was embarrassing as Sir William had already submitted his paper to the Royal Commission, who had approved of it. But the Bank's opinion was reinforced by that of John Portal, who not only agreed with their views in regard to colour, but added that the time taken in manufacture would be so much longer that a very large increase of staff and plant would be necessary in order to keep up the supply. Apart from the loss of security which the engagement of a large number of strangers would involve, the consequent in-crease of cost would double the price of the paper, and as it was heavier than the paper then in use, the duty payable upon it would be greater. In the circumstances, the Bank had no alternative but to inform Sir William Congreve that they were unable to adopt his invention.

It is a matter of interest that, although Sir William Con-greve's inventions were not adopted by the Bank, both of them were subsequently taken into use. In a 'Notice', issued by him and dated 1 March 1821, the attention of the country bankers was invited to the fact that his colour-printing device had been adopted by the Government for the production of stamps, which would shortly be issued from the Stamp Office. The duty stamps were, at that time, impressed upon the backs of the notes, and it was maintained that the new process would provide an effec-tive measure of security. In the same notice, the country bankers were informed that his 'triple paper', which would afford further security for their notes, might be obtained at the 'New Bank Note Paper Office for the Prevention of

[1] Dard Hunter, *Papermaking*, pp. 283-8.

Forgery', which Sir William Congreve had opened 'with the immediate sanction of the Government', at Somerset House.

In the meantime, there had been no abatement in the number of forgeries, which still stood at 31,000, and the Bank was subjected to constant criticism of what was considered to be its ineffective attempts to stem the tide. Among the critics was David Ricardo, who appeared in that role for a special reason. For some years before, Ricardo had been maintaining that the depreciation of bank-notes was due to their over-issue, following the release of the Bank from the obligation to pay gold on demand. To put an end to the depreciation, he advocated the restoration of convertibility, but, realising that rapid restoration of a full gold coinage would create unnecessary difficulties, he produced his 'Ingot Plan' in which he urged that the notes should be made convertible, not into specie, but into bullion.[1] The plan met with a large measure of approval—its principles were, in fact, embodied in the Act of 1819 for the gradual resumption of cash payments —but there was also considerable opposition. The Bank was in favour of the resumption of cash payments as soon as possible, and the public were growing weary of the continued circulation of forged notes. The adoption of the ingot plan would have entailed the retention of the small notes, of which they were anxious to be rid, and the difficulties of preventing the forgery of these notes loomed large in the arguments of the opposition. Ricardo's reaction to this argument was to range him prominently among the critics of the Bank's alleged lack of success in reducing the number of forgeries. He suggested that the Bank could deal with the problem if it tried, and implied that it was not trying. But we who have followed the

[1] It was, in fact, the procedure that was adopted in 1925.

deliberations of the committees concerned, and the Bank's collaboration with the Royal Commission, may think that the criticism was, perhaps, ill-founded.

The general public, meanwhile, continued to voice their indignation at the increasing number of executions. It will be appreciated that the Bank, too, were distressed at the number of capital convictions, and for some time past had been doing all that was possible to reduce them. They had taken advantage of a clause in the Act of 1801, by which the offence of 'being in possession of forged Notes' was punishable by transportation, to secure from the accused a plea of guilty on this minor charge, in order to avoid the capital sentence which conviction on the major charge of uttering forged notes would entail. In February 1819, however, it was pointed out by Lord Sidmouth that the practice of inducing a person to confess the guilt of one offence by the threat of prosecution for another was a flagrant impropriety and even compromised the royal pre-rogative,[1] with the result that, after that date, this humani-tarian practice, which had saved the lives of a great number of people, was discontinued.

Early in 1819, there was an upward surge in the wave of public indignation, on the appearance of an etching by Gorge Cruikshank, which he called his 'Bank Note—not to be imitated'. The etching was exposed for sale in the shop of William Hone, the bookseller of 45 Ludgate Hill, and the crowds that pressed to see and to purchase it were so great as to form an obstruction to the traffic. As will be seen (Plate XI), the design was of a horrific character, in which the attributes of execution, transportation and prison life were graphically portrayed, with a vignette de-picting a Moloch-like Britannia engaged in devouring an infant, and the supposititious signature of 'Jack Ketch', the

[1] W. Marston Acres, *The Bank of England from Within*, p. 342.

popular designation of the common hangman. In later years Cruikshank claimed that, after the appearance of his 'Bank Note—not to be imitated', the Bank 'issued no more one pound notes, and so there was no more hanging for passing one pound notes; not only that, but ultimately no hanging even for forgery'.[1] Such a consummation would have been a great achievement, but, unfortunately, the claim was unfounded. Notes for £1 continued to be issued for a further two years, and although convictions diminished in number, the diminution was due to a policy which the Bank had adopted of refraining, in many instances, from prosecution. Moreover, it was not until 1832, when this etching might well have been forgotten, that the crime of forgery was no longer punishable by death.[2] But Cruikshank was inclined to make such claims, and, as Jerrold states in his biography, 'had a habit of overestimating the effect of his work, as well as his share in any enterprise in which he had a part', as was evidenced by his pretension that the picaresque portions, if not the whole, of *Oliver Twist* were inspired by him, and that Dickens merely wrote the story round his drawings.[3]

In February 1820, the Royal Commission issued their second and final report. They had little to add to their earlier report, except to record that they had given further consideration to 'another plan of great ingenuity', which had already been laid before them on several occasions. There can be little doubt that the plan referred to was that of Jacob Perkins, but the further consideration thus given to it would appear to have been of no avail, for the Commission were unable to recommend its adoption. They gave

[1] Blanchard Jerrold, *The Life of George Cruikshank*, I, p. 93.

[2] W. Marston Acres, *op. cit.* p. 346.

[3] Blanchard Jerrold, *op. cit.* chapter VIII; John Forster, *The Life of Charles Dickens*, pp. 112, 117, 475-6.

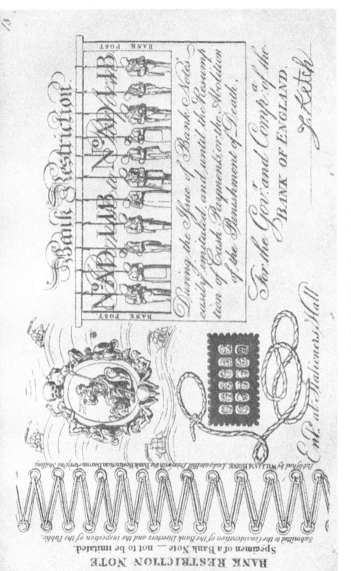

XI. George Cruikshank's bank restriction note.
Actual size 5 in. × 8 in.

whole-hearted support, however, to Applegarth and Cowper, whom they now mentioned by name, and referred to improvements that had, at the suggestion of the Commission, been made to their plan. During this year, Applegarth and Cowper continued to work at the Bank on the production of their notes,[1] while Charles Heath was assiduous in keeping the work of his firm constantly in the mind of the Bank. William Bawtree had succeeded J. H. Harper, on his retirement in the previous year, and there now fell to him the laborious task of imitating by hand the intricacies of machine engraving, which was the outstanding feature of Perkins's system, but in order to render this task less laborious, he had set to work on the construction of a lathe, by which the work would be done mechanically. Heath did not fail to criticise Bawtree's imitations, but he also expressed appreciation of the skill with which they were executed. He pointed out, however, that the Bank's engraver, with all the resources at his command, was in a position to produce better work than the forger, at whose defeat they were aiming, and who would be working under many disadvantages. In April 1821, Heath had a long interview with the Governor, at which he stressed the advantages—and there were indeed many—of Perkins's system, but, after a final conversation in August of the same year, he was informed that, although the Bank was open to consider further specimens, he could be given no encouragement to submit them or to incur any further expenses for the prosecution of his plans.

For some time past, the Bank had reported to the

[1] It would appear that the Bank were impressed by Applegarth and Cowper's insistence upon secrecy, for they applied the principle to the whole of the department, when in 1820 the Superintendent of the Printing Office was directed 'to admit no person into that Office or to view any part of the Business thereof . . . without an order in writing from the Governor or Deputy Governor for the time being'.

Government on more than one occasion, that their stocks of gold would permit of the resumption of cash payments, with the result that, in May 1821, an Act of Parliament was passed by which the restriction was brought to an end. The issue of notes for £1 and £2 then ceased, but Applegarth and Cowper continued with their work on the notes of higher denominations. At the same time, Bawtree concentrated on his task of imitating them, until there ensued what might be described as a duel between Applegarth and Cowper, and Bawtree, with colours as the chosen weapons. Having produced a successful imitation of a note in two colours, Bawtree would be confronted with another, in which three colours appeared, and so the contest continued until a note in five colours had been successfully imitated. The end, however, came suddenly, when on 13 September 1821 it was resolved that 'in the opinion of the Committee, Mr Bawtree's imitation is quite fatal to Messrs. Applegarth & Cowper's Note', and the firm were informed accordingly. On the cessation of their work, the Bank paid compensation to the partners themselves and to a number of people who had been specially employed upon this experiment, the total cost of which had amounted to more than £40,000, and which left upon the Bank's hands a useless stock of four million notes.

Thus ended the search for the inimitable note, which had lasted for twenty-five years, and of which the only material outcome had been the adoption in 1801 of Brewer's watermark embodying the waved lines.

CHAPTER V

THE BANK OF ENGLAND NOTE
FROM 1822 TO 1854

DURING THE year 1822, when the tumult and the shouting attendant upon the anti-forgery campaign had died away, and the notes for £1 and £2 that were still in circulation were gradually becoming fewer, the Bank seems to have reviewed the general bank-note position and to have decided to discontinue the issue of notes of certain denominations which had served their turn and were deemed to be no longer necessary. The notes for £15, which, when they had been introduced in 1759, had done much to relieve the pressing shortage of currency at that time, were discontinued, as were also those for £25, which had served a like purpose when they were first issued in 1765. The notes in circulation in 1822 were, therefore, those of £5, £10, £20, £30, £40, £50, £100, £200, £300, £500 and £1000, a series that remained unaltered for a number of years.

In the same year, a grant of £2000 was made to John Portal in respect of the expenses that he had incurred during the preceding four years in carrying out a number of experiments, some at the Bank's request and some on his own initiative. It was the outcome of one of the last named that formed the basis of a plan which he now submitted to the Bank and which involved a radical change in the design of the bank-note watermark. When in 1801 the waved lines and the denomination in words had been em-

bodied in the watermark of the £1 and £2 notes, the
remainder of the design, namely the looped border and
scroll in the dexter margin had remained unchanged. The
proposal now under consideration was to dispense with
both of these features, and to substitute a broad and simple
design of waved lines, enclosed in a panel with waved
edges, covering the whole expanse of the paper except for
a very narrow margin. The denomination of the note concerned was to be shown in roman capitals similar to those
that had been used for the notes of £1 and £2, and in the
same place, that is to say, across the middle of the note.
The words BANK OF ENGLAND were to appear, also in
large roman capitals, at the head and the foot of the panel,
and, by increasing almost imperceptibly the thickness of
the paper, it was possible to make more prominent both
the waved lines and the lettering. The clarity of the watermark and the simplicity of the design earned the immediate
approval of the Bank, who straightway decided to adopt
it, but it was not until 1824 that sufficient paper had been
manufactured and notes printed to enable an issue to be
made. In February of that year the public were notified
by an advertisement in the *London Gazette* that notes
printed on the new paper would be issued on 1 March, and
particulars were given of the manner in which it would
differ from the paper then in use. Notes of all denominations would show the panel of waved lines and the words
BANK OF ENGLAND but only those of £5 to £50 would
bear the denomination in words; it was not until 1887 that
the paper for notes of £100 to £1000 was so distinguished.
At the same time it was announced that the year of issue,
which, since 1810, had been printed after the heading
'Bank of England' would be discontinued. There was no
doubt that the new watermark was a great improvement
upon the old one. It continued in use for the next thirty

years when it became the basis of the design which succeeded it and which remains in use to this day.

The practice that had been adopted in 1810 of printing
some of the notes four on a sheet appears to have been discontinued when the issue of notes for £1 and £2 ceased.
The paper was, however, made on an even larger mould of
the size of eight notes, and by an ingenious arrangement
of the mould, the paper, although 'couched' as one sheet,
was divisible on being dried into four sheets of the size of
two notes. Thus, each note had its traditional three deckle
edges. But the custom seems to have continued of reckon-
ing in double reams of four notes to a sheet, for when the
paper situation was reviewed at the introduction of the new
watermark, the reams were referred to as double reams,
containing 1920 (480 × 4) notes. Incidentally, it was
agreed at the same time that the price of a double ream
should remain unchanged at 32s. 6d., that the said ream
should weigh 4 lb. 2 oz. with a tolerance of two ounces
more or less, and that, as a standard of strength, a single
sheet, folded eight times, should be capable of supporting
a weight of 35 lb.

It will be appreciated that reams of 480 sheets were inappropriate to the printing of bank-notes, since they were
required in thousands, and that it was necessary to add a
further twenty sheets to each ream in order to complete
1000 notes. Nevertheless, the paper continued to be so
delivered until 1836, when the Deputy Governor suggested
that it might be made up at the mills into reams of 500
sheets. John Portal was agreeable to the proposal but he
pointed out that permission would have to be obtained
from the Board of Excise, since 'the Law directs that 20
quires with 24 sheets in each quire are to make a ream'.
The necessary permission was apparently obtained, for
later in the same year the paper was delivered in 'reams' of

500 sheets, a practice which has continued to the present day.

The Bank's stock of gold, which in 1821 had made possible the resumption of cash payments, had been more than adequate to meet normal demands until, by reason of the export of bullion and an internal demand that had arisen in consequence of a wave of speculation that had swept over the country, a serious drain had been made upon it. Towards the latter part of 1825 the failure of a number of banks, and the financial crisis that ensued, led to a run upon the Bank of England and to a further reduction of the already diminished stock of gold. So great was the demand for currency that there was a shortage even of notes, and the £1 note was again called in to relieve the situation. Not to any great extent, however, for the relief was supplied by a stock of £1 notes, to the value of approximately £1,000,000, which had been left over from the days of the restriction, and which had remained unissued in the vaults of the Bank.[1] The notes were plate-printed on the 'old' paper with the looped border, and were unnumbered and undated, but the required process was speedily carried out by the Bank's printers, so that the notes were ready for issue on 16 December.[2] The relief provided by the release of this hoard was welcome but transient, for by Saturday the 17th, the Bank had run out of notes for £5 and £10. Once again the printers were called upon, and on the following day, Sunday the 18th, a stock of notes of these much-needed denominations was available.[3] The panic gradually subsided, and by Christmas the immediate crisis was over, but the financial condition of the country had

[1] Sir John Clapham, *The Bank of England; a History*, vol. II, p. 100.
[2] The form of these notes was curiously contradictory, for, while the surface-printed date line read 1825, the plate printed year at the head of the note was that of its first printing, namely 1821.
[3] Sir John Clapham, *op. cit.* vol. II, p. 100.

received a severe blow, the recovery from which was a long and painful process.

Incidental to the crisis of 1825, was the failure of a number of country banks, whose stability had been insufficient to withstand the persistent demand upon them to meet their notes, which in many instances had been gravely over-issued, and one of the steps taken to amend the state of the country's finances was to strengthen the position of the country banking system. It will be remembered that, by an Act of 1709, no organisation of more than six persons had been allowed to practice banking, but in 1826 an Act of Parliament was passed permitting the establishment of joint-stock banks, provided that they did not operate within sixty-five miles of London. A similar plan had been adopted in Ireland by legislation in 1821, the limit in that instance having been fifty miles from Dublin, and it is interesting to note that, although differing numerically, the two distances were to all intents and purposes the same, since sixty-five English miles were approximately equivalent to fifty Irish miles.[1] With a view to strengthening still further the country banking system, the Bank of England was empowered by the same Act to establish branches at any place in England, a course of action that had been proposed on many previous occasions, but had not been adopted. No time was lost, however, in putting the scheme into practice, and a committee which had been appointed in January 1826 had, by April of that year, formulated a plan for the establishment and direction of such branches. Again no time was lost, and on 19 July 1826 the first of the Bank's country branches was opened at Gloucester.

Other branches followed in quick succession at Manchester, Swansea, Birmingham, Liverpool, Bristol, Leeds, Exeter, Newcastle, Hull and Norwich, while a few years

[1] F. G. Hall, *The Bank of Ireland*, 1783-1946, p. 135.

later, branches were established at Plymouth, Portsmouth and Leicester.[1] One of the first recommendations made by the responsible committee was to the effect that each branch should circulate its own notes, printed upon the paper then in use. The notes were to be plainly marked with the name of the branch by which they were issued, and were to be payable only at that branch, but later, when the final regulations were formulated, it was decided that the notes should be payable in London as well as at the branch of origin. As each branch opened, a supply of notes had to be printed for its use, and a method was adopted whereby a sudden demand for notes from a particular branch might be met with the minimum of disturbance. The plate-printed portion of the notes was the same for all branches and identical with those issued in London, except that the words 'here or in London' were engraved below the lines 'I promise to pay', etc., while the name of the branch appeared only in the letterpress date line, between the two dates. It was decided that there should be no branch issue of notes for £200, £300, or £1000;[2] otherwise, the denominations were the same as those issued by the head office. In later years, when branches were opened in London, first at Burlington Gardens and then at the Law Courts, no special notes were printed for their use, and the method by which the branch notes were distinguished was the cause of some confusion, which led, on an occasion that can be recalled, to a stormy protest by a solicitor, who had hurried into the Law Courts branch in order to cash a note of one of the Bank's country branches,

[1] Many of these branches were closed as they became redundant. The Bank now has branches only at Manchester, Birmingham, Liverpool, Bristol, Leeds, Newcastle and Southampton. These branches now issue 'London' notes, the separate issue of branch notes having ceased in 1939.

[2] An issue of £1000 notes was, in fact, made by the Hull branch in 1882, but it was short-lived and ceased in 1889.

and who refused, with indignation, to accept the decision that a journey to Threadneedle Street was necessary, or that, for the purposes of the Bank's note issue, the Law Courts branch was not 'in London'.

Early in 1831, the Bank heard again from Jacob Perkins, whose method of bank-note printing had been rejected ten years before, but, on this occasion, he appeared in a new role. The business of bank-note engraving and printing that he had established in 1819 had soon run smoothly and could be left to the able direction of his partner Charles Heath—Gideon Fairman had returned to Philadelphia in 1822—while Perkins was free to seek another outlet for his inventive ability. He found it in an entirely different branch of industry, and had, in partnership with his son A. M. Perkins, become a pioneer in the development of appliances for the use of hot water and steam, under pressure, for heating and other purposes. It was in this capacity that he now approached the Bank with a plan for heating the engraved printing plates by means of a hot-water apparatus, instead of by the charcoal stoves which were then in use and which were admittedly productive of unhealthy working conditions. In May 1831 William Bawtree, who had investigated the scheme, reported favourably upon it, and the installation of a trial apparatus was decided upon, with a view to testing its efficiency. While the trial was in progress, expert opinion was taken, and 'Dr Birkbeck, Professor Faraday and other scientific gentlemen'[1] were called into consultation. Faraday recommended

[1] George Birkbeck, M.D., although a practising physician, is better known as the originator of the movement for establishing mechanics' institutions. In later years, the institution which he had founded in London was named Birkbeck College in memory of its founder, and now forms part of the University of London. Michael Faraday, then director of the laboratory of the Royal Institution, is chiefly remembered on account of his work as a pioneer of electrical research and discovery.

G

the addition of a pressure gauge, and, as a further safe-guard, thermometers to take the temperature of the water on leaving and entering the boiler, after which, the experts declared the apparatus to be effective and, 'with the exercise of moderate caution', to be safe from explosion.

It was, accordingly, decided to adopt the plan for the whole of the twenty-six presses then in use, at a cost of twelve guineas for each press, the Bank having been impressed by the 'advantage to the Workmen being enabled to pursue their occupation in a purer atmosphere than as at present by the use of Charcoal', to say nothing of the saving that was forecast of two-thirds of the cost of fuel. The system would seem, however, to have been not wholly free from fault, for in the following year the Bank had to deal with a complaint from the pressmen, in regard to the temperature achieved, in which complaint they were supported by J. S. Bawtree, who was now acting as superintendent, his brother William having died in the previous year. It would appear, too, that one of the pipes of the apparatus had burst. Faraday, who had been retained to undertake periodical inspections of the installation, was, however, undisturbed. He was satisfied with the explanation of the manufacturer in regard to the burst pipe, and asserted that the apparatus would give 'heat enough and quick enough' provided that proper attention was paid to the plant. It would seem that the necessary attention was thenceforth given, for we hear no more of the subject.

In 1832, an event occurred which led to a material change in the method of printing the Bank of England notes, for in that year the Deputy Governor, while on a visit to Ireland, was given the opportunity of inspecting the printing department of the Bank of Ireland, and was greatly impressed by the 'simplicity, neatness, and perfection' of the methods employed. John Oldham, who, it will

be remembered, was appointed engineer and chief engraver to the Bank of Ireland in 1812, still occupied that
position, and had, during the intervening twenty years,
introduced a number of additions and improvements to
the system with which he had started. The Deputy
Governor on his return reported his high opinion of the
process to the Governor, and there ensued a correspondence with the Bank of Ireland on the subject of their
method of printing and the possibility of its adoption by
the Bank of England. Oldham's advice was taken and a
preliminary estimate of the cost of the installation was prepared by him, which convinced the Bank that not only was
the system eminently suitable for their work, but also that
its adoption would lead to a material reduction of the cost
of note production. It was agreed, therefore, that J. S.
Bawtree and his assistant should go to Dublin in order to inspect and report upon the system, taking with them a number of sheets of Bank of England note paper in order that
trial proofs might be printed upon them, and the suitability
of the Bank's paper for use on Oldham's press determined.

The two officials returned with the required proofs, and
reported their approval of the system. They expressed particular admiration of Oldham's numbering machine, which
it will be remembered, was entirely mechanical and did
not necessitate the constant manhandling required by the
machine that the Bank were then using. Unfortunately,
the report has little to say about the plate transfer press, by
which identical printing plates were produced from a
master plate by means of rollers. This press is referred to
as Oldham's invention, and he was indeed responsible for
much of the mechanism, but a comparison of his machine
with that of Jacob Perkins shows that, although they
differed in many respects, the principle upon which they
worked was the same. The method of damping the paper

before printing was considerably in advance of that usually employed, namely the passing of three or four sheets at a time through a trough of water, after which they were stacked to be ready for printing upon on the following day. Oldham's damping device consisted of a container, capable of being sealed, into which from 1000 to 5000 sheets of paper were placed. Water was admitted, the container sealed, and the air exhausted in order to produce a partial vacuum. The water was thus enabled to penetrate between the sheets, which in fifteen minutes were thoroughly damped and ready for printing, if necessary, half an hour later.

The printing presses would appear to have been of the old flat-bed type, but they were driven by power derived from a steam engine, ensuring, in spite of the fact that the inking, wiping and polishing had still to be done by hand, a measure of physical relief to the pressmen and a considerable increase in the speed of production. The Bank, at that time, were using 24 presses, each press manned by one printer producing approximately 1500 notes per day, and it was estimated that the Bank's requirements could be supplied by seven of Oldham's presses, each of which, with three men to a press, would produce approximately 4000 notes per day. The report went on to say that after 100 sheets (200 notes) had been printed they were placed in a shallow tray and inserted by one of the pressmen through a narrow aperture into a device known as the 'receiver'. The aperture closed immediately and another below it opened automatically to release a further 100 unprinted sheets with which the printer returned to the press. The receiver was situated against the wall of the room, and, on the other side of the wall, in the office, the trays were extracted, the sheets counted and placed between millboards for drying. The steam supply, which had already been used for heating the printing plates and

driving the presses, was again employed in the drying process, which was of a most ingenious nature and resembled
the modern process of air-conditioning. A further security
device was employed to record the number of sheets
printed. It will be remembered that, when it was first invented, the numbering device was attached to presses
where it was not required for numbering, in order to
record the number of sheets printed. Oldham had improved upon this practice, and had invented a system
whereby, by means of light chains, running from each
press to a recording instrument at the end of the room, the
security staff were enabled to note and to keep an account
of the number of impressions printed by each machine, in
order that the figure might be agreed with that of the output at the end of the day.

A select committee, which had been appointed to consider the proposal to adopt Oldham's system, held consultations with Bawtree on the details of his report, and
recommended that the Bank of Ireland might be asked to
allow Oldham to come to London in order to inspect the
Bank's printing department and to advise further on the
matter. The visit was arranged and Oldham was able to set
at rest any doubts as to the advisability of adopting his
method. Before coming to a decision, however, the Bank
considered that it would be wise to take the opinion of
certain 'eminent scientific and practical gentlemen', and
the services of 'Mr Babbage, Mr Brunel, Mr Donkin and
Mr Field'[1] were enlisted, with the request that they should

---

[1] Charles Babbage, F.R.S., the eminent mathematician and
mechanician. Marc Isambard Brunel, the distinguished civil and
mechanical engineer, was knighted in 1841; he was the father of I. K.
Brunel, the famous engineer of the Great Western Railway. Bryan
Donkin, an engineer of outstanding ability with many inventions to
his credit. Joshua Field, an expert engineer and vice-president of the
Institution of Civil Engineers of which he was a founder.

inspect and report upon the system. Their approval was unanimous, and the Bank decided to install the necessary plant and machinery,[1] which Oldham had recommended, and in respect of which he had prepared detailed estimates of cost. The preliminary negotiations, the consideration of reports and the travelling to and from Ireland had taken some time, and it was not until 1835 that this decision was reached, whereupon further negotiations took place with the Bank of Ireland as to the possibility of their parting with the services of Oldham, in order that he might enter the service of the Bank and superintend the new installation. The Bank of Ireland were agreeable, and Oldham, who was then fifty-seven years of age, left his native Dublin to be appointed, on 24 March 1836, 'Mechanical Engineer and Principal of the Engraving, Plate Printing, Numbering and Dating Office',[2] at a salary of £1000 per annum, with a preliminary gratuity of £5000 as compensation for his having moved from Dublin. Oldham was given six months in which to complete the installation of his plant and machinery, and later in the year it was possible to begin printing according to the new method. The Bank were undoubtedly the gainers. The total cost of the installation was £10,500, while an annual saving of approximately £7000 was foreseen; the pressmen were relieved of the exhausting labour of turning the cross of the press at each impression, and above all the Bank of England notes had acquired, by the use of the plate transfer press, that essential quality of a note issue—identity.

The appearance of the new notes was identical with that

[1] The steam engine that had been installed in 1819 for Applegarth and Cowper was used, but in 1843 the Bank purchased a new Boulton and Watt beam engine, which remained in use until 1904.

[2] J. S. Bawtree remained as superintendent until his retirement in 1838.

of those that they replaced, except in regard to the manner of numbering. Oldham's machine, which had originally printed the numbers as 'No. - - - - 1' and so on, now printed them in the manner in use today, '00001' and so on, thereby increasing still further the protection against the risk of alteration. The machine also embodied an improvement, which had been adopted by the Bank of Ireland a few years before, namely, the discontinuation of the not very necessary 'No.' before the numbers, and the substitution of a cipher. Each date, in respect of which 100,000 notes were printed, had its own cipher—a further trap for the forger—which consisted, at first, of two roman capital letters arranged one above the other. It will be perceived that the possible combinations of two letters were limited, and it was necessary to change, from time to time, the form of the letters. The first change took place in 1844, when italic capital letters were substituted for the roman, and in subsequent years the changes were rung by the adoption of different forms of lettering until 1869, when figures were introduced, producing a vast increase in the number of possible combinations. Letters and figures in conjunction have continued to be used until the present day, changes having been made, from time to time, in order to ensure that no cipher is repeated until sufficient time has elapsed to remove the danger of confusion.

Having now instituted by the use of the plate transfer press, a system which secured identity in the notes, the Bank again considered the possibility of a change of design, and in 1838 a committee was appointed to consider whether any improvement or alteration might be made in the note as it then was. The committee, which consisted of the Deputy Governor and four directors under the chairmanship of the Governor, was appointed on 26 April 1838, but it was not until September of that year that they were called upon to meet. At this meeting, the Governor explained that the delay was due, in the first place, to his having gone deeply into the subject with a view to deciding whether the then existing note provided sufficient security to the public, and, having satisfied himself as to the notes' shortcomings, to consider the best means of providing the required degree of security. Moreover, he was anxious that the committee should not suffer the embarrassments experienced by their predecessors of the committees of 1802-17, due to the spate of inadequate proposals that they had been called upon to consider,[1] and to that end he had consulted 'Mr Wyon, Mr Corbould and Mr LeKeux',[2] with a view to the production of a new design.

The foundation upon which they built was the oft-recommended principle of a combination of the arts—it will be remembered that this principle was first suggested by Jeremy Bentham in 1800—and the design was specially planned to include no less than five different methods of engraving, which no single person, however skilled, would be able to reproduce. A sketch by Corbould of the proposed design was submitted to the committee, who appointed a sub-committee to sit in an advisory capacity. The sub-committee consisted of William Wyon, Henry Corbould, H. LeKeux, J. H. Robinson,[3] C. R. Cockerell,[4] and John Oldham. The sub-committee evolved and considered no less than nine variations of the original sketch,

[1] See p. 49 above.

[2] William Wyon, R.A., designer of coins and medals at the Royal Mint. Henry Corbould, a distinguished painter, chiefly remembered for his drawings of ancient marbles. Henry LeKeux, line engraver, a younger brother of the equally notable John LeKeux.

[3] J. H. Robinson (R.A. in 1867), a versatile engraver noted for the peculiar richness of his line.

[4] C. R. Cockerell, F.R.S., R.A., architect to the Bank, had a profound knowledge of classical art derived from extensive travels in Greece and the Aegean.

but they worked quickly, and on 13 December, they recommended the adoption of the design that represented the final outcome of their labours. As will be seen from the reproduction of their sketch (Plate XII), the design was elaborate and impressive, the text of the note, which was to be in the finest script engraving, being surrounded by a variety of engraved figures and devices. The vignette at the head of the design, depicting the Pleiades, which was adapted from one of Flaxman's drawings in illustration of the poems of Hesiod, was to be stipple engraved by Robinson, who was also to execute the line engraving of the figures of Mercury and Fortune (representing Commerce and Abundance) at the foot of the note, and the repeated figure of Britannia which was derived from a statue of Juno, then in the entrance hall of the Royal Academy. The repeated sums were to be on a background of rose engine engraving, while the elaborate border, which incorporated representations of two beehives as emblems of industry— the 'bank of mony' had long since been forgotten—and the heads of William and Mary, under whose auspices the Bank had been founded, were to be reproduced by the recently invented method of medallion engraving from models in relief,[1] the work of William Wyon.

On its submission to the Court of Directors in January 1839, the design did not meet with unqualified approval. A number of directors expressed the view that the choice offered to the Court was too restricted, in that they had no alternative but to accept or reject a single proposal, and suggested that a number of designs should be submitted by other artists, in order that a selection might be made.

[1] Medallion engraving was effected by a machine invented by Achille Collas in 1830, in which a point known as the 'feeler' was passed backwards and forwards over a model in low relief, and was linked to an engraving point which followed each of its movements, producing on a flat surface the appearance of the original relief.

Some very constructive criticisms were made by William Cotton,[1] who agreed that there should be a wider choice and recommended that Sir Francis Chantrey, Sir Augustus Callcott and other celebrated artists might be taken into consultation. He was of the opinion, too, that the figure of Britannia should be depicted in the traditional attitude, as on the Bank's seal, that is to say, seated, and at the same time, he criticised the figure itself, in that it was too war-like. He deplored, also, the lack of homogeneity in the design, which he described as 'a picture with a note in the middle of it'. During the following three years, successive Special Committees worked on the subject, but there is no record of their having considered alternative designs. Examples of some of these, however, still exist, notably a delightful design by Sir Richard Westmacott, the sculptor, in respect of which he was paid a fee of £150. But the records are concerned only with the development of the original proposal, in the course of which a difficulty arose from the fact that some of Robinson's engraving was so delicate that it failed to 'raise' a satisfactory relief on the soft steel roller of the plate transfer press, and Thomas Oldham[2] was obliged to ask him to deepen his work. Robinson's reaction to this request is not recorded, but it is significant that the difficulty was overcome by Oldham's making an improvement to the press. Other difficulties were encountered and overcome, but to no avail, for in March 1842 when the matter was again considered by the Court of Directors, they decided that they were 'not prepared at present to adopt the new Note, but deem it expedient to

[1] William Cotton, who became Governor in 1842, was the inventor of the gold-weighing machine, whereby sovereigns were weighed individually and the light coins separated automatically from the remainder.

[2] Thomas Oldham, the eldest of John Oldham's seventeen children, had succeeded his father who had died in 1840.

XII. Sketch for a note proposed in 1838

give the subject of the improvement of the present Note further consideration'. Thus ended the second attempt to change the design of the Bank of England note.

One of the criticisms voiced by the Governor in 1838 had concerned the watermark of the then existing note, which he considered to be easily imitated by any one of the methods well known to forgers, and recommended that, while the design of the watermark should remain otherwise unchanged, the denomination across the middle of the note should be in opaque letters instead of being only outlined. William Brewer, the Bank's mould maker and John Dusautoy, who had been John Portal's manager since the death of William Bridges in 1819, were consulted as to the possibility of producing this effect, and they agreed that such paper could be made. It is not known what progress they made in this connection, but it is significant that, in the report of the committee in December 1838, it was stated that no recommendation had been made to introduce this improvement in the paper, as in order to do so a new process would be required. The reason is not far to seek when the method of producing a watermark is considered.[1]

A sheet of paper was consistently of the same degree of opacity except in places where the wire design had made the paper thinner, but by no manipulation of wires could a part of the sheet be made thicker. A new method was indeed required, but it was not entirely new, for attention had already been given to the problem by French papermakers. As far back as 1812, the old-established firm of Johannot at Annonay had succeeded in producing such an effect by making a depression in a 'wove' mould, so that more pulp would remain in it and produce, as it were, a third plane of a greater degree of opacity than the

[1] See p. 9 above.

remainder of the sheet.[1] This early attempt was nothing more than a simple oval framework, enclosing an ordinary wire portrait watermark, but it was a beginning, and, although there is little to be learned of the development of this method,[2] we know that in 1843 it had reached a much higher standard, for in that year an engraving of a proposed new Bank of England note was submitted by a French firm, printed upon paper, called by the maker 'papier filigrané inimitable', which provided not only the third plane, but also intermediate shades and middle tones. The watermark of this specimen consisted of a large representation of the royal arms, occupying the whole of the paper, and was probably produced by subjecting the wove wire mould to pressure between a wood-block cut in relief and a counterpart moulded from it, so that the pulp would lie in varying thicknesses and produce an effect of light and shade in the finished paper. Although this watermark provided the very effect that the Bank had desired, but had abandoned for lack of means to produce it, surprisingly little regard seems to have been paid to the specimens that were submitted. The Bank's attitude is reflected in a letter written by Thomas Oldham to John Portal in March 1845. It would appear that Wyndham Portal, who had become assistant to his father in 1841, had discussed specimens of this paper with Oldham and asked him to send them to his father for inspection. In the letter accompanying the specimens, Oldham stated that, on their having been submitted to the French Government, they had been referred to in the Chamber of Deputies as of importance, but that they had been submitted also to the Bank of Austria 'where

---

[1] Dard Hunter, *Papermaking*, p. 295.
[2] The records of the French paper-makers likely to have taken part in this development have been destroyed in one or other of the three intervening wars.

they received no attention'. It would appear that a similar fate attended their submission to the Bank of England, where, according to Oldham, 'they died a very early death.'

There was, however, one person who took the shaded watermark seriously. William Brewer, who had been the Bank's mouldmaker for forty-five years, and who is stated to have been 'aged and infirm', refused to give up the quest, and, in collaboration with John Smith, a die-sinker of Upper Fountain Place, City Road, he evolved a method of watermarking by incorporating in the mould thin brass plates, die-stamped with the required design and perforated in order to allow the surplus water to drain from the pulp. The two inventors proceeded with the perfection of their device, which they patented in 1849, and two years later they received adequate recognition of their work, when, on 8 May 1851 an agreement was sealed between the Bank and 'Messrs Brewer, Smith & Co.', by which the Bank acquired the sole right to use the invention. But we must leave the shaded watermark at this point and consider another development that was to affect, in no small degree, the printing of the Bank of England note.

The development of the science of electricity in its early days had been a slow process, but during the first half of the nineteenth century, the progress made was extensive and swift. The discovery of the electric cell at the end of the preceding century, and the work of Michael Faraday on the subject of electrolysis had made possible the electrodeposition of metal and the development of electrotyping, in which metal is deposited upon a mould, taken from an original plate, engraved in recess or relief, and produces upon its surface a perfect reproduction of the original. The improvement of the first Galvanic and Voltaic cells had been the subject of much study and research by successive experimentalists, and among them was Dr Alfred

Smee, whose grandfather had been in the service of the Bank and whose father, William Smee, was now Chief Accountant. While he was a medical student, Alfred Smee lived at the Bank in the official quarters allotted to his father, where, like the great Galvani before him, he combined his medical studies with experiments in electricity. The Bank at that time had no official medical officer, and after Smee had received his diploma from the Royal College of Surgeons in 1840 and had set up as a consultant in Finsbury Square, he was employed by the Bank whenever medical advice was required.[1] In 1840, his electrical experiments culminated in the production of an improved cell, which he called his 'Chemico-Mechanical Battery', but which was usually referred to as the 'Smee Cell'. In the same year, he was awarded, in recognition of his invention, the Isis Gold Medal of the Royal Society of Arts, and in a paper which he read on the occasion of its presentation, he told his audience how he had set out to construct a battery which could be used at a moment's notice, have considerable power, be cheap to produce and which would not need laborious cleaning after use. The invention was taken into use extensively by industrialists, and in recognition of his valuable contribution to electrical science, Smee was in 1841 elected a Fellow of the Royal Society at the early age of twenty-three years. The steadiness of the current produced by the Smee Cell made it particularly suitable for the electro-deposition of metal, and Smee, who had made a special study of electro-metallurgy, became especially interested in the production of electrotypes.

There can be no doubt that the idea of printing the Bank of England notes from electrotypes in relief, instead of by plate-printing from plates engraved in recess, was

[1] Smee was appointed the first medical officer to the Bank of England in 1857.

originated by Smee. He was constantly in and out of the
Bank, and would have had ample opportunity of discussing
with the officials of the printing department his firm belief
in the efficacy of surface printing and the use of electrotypes. It cannot be thought that Thomas Oldham, bred
and brought up in an atmosphere of engraving and plate-
printing, would take readily to any suggestion of this kind,
but Oldham died in 1851, and in November of that year,
Smee laid before the Governor his reasons for advocating
that 'surface printing from electrotypes could be advan-
tageously employed for Bank of England Notes'. The
Governor was interested in the proposal, and arranged that
Smee should consult with Oldham's successors, Henry
Hensman, who was now engineer, and John Coe, the
Superintendent of the Bank-note Printing and Stationery
Office, with a view to giving the process a trial by using it
for the printing of cheques. Hensman and Coe were found
to be ready collaborators, and, after the surface printing of
cheques had proved a success, they continued to work, in
conjunction with Smee, on his plan to print the bank-notes
by the same means.

An initial setback arose from the difficulty of finding
engravers who would undertake the unusual work of cutting a relief out of solid metal, and, when finally two were
found, they agreed to undertake the work only if it were
first of all engraved in recess, presumably to provide the
necessary copy. It was arranged, therefore, that J. H.
Robinson[1] should engrave the new vignette, which was then
cut in relief out of steel by John Thompson, the veteran
engraver who at that time was nearly seventy years of age.
The remainder of the note was engraved by the Bank's
engravers, and the reliefs cut in copper by John Skirving,
who, as a typefounder's punch-cutter, was skilled in such

---

[1] See p. 92 n.

work. Much thought was given to the choice of the best method by which to take moulds of the original reliefs. Gutta percha, wax and lead were all considered for this purpose, but the electrically minded Smee preferred to produce moulds by electro-deposition on the originals, and this method was used except for the vignette—cut, it will be remembered, in steel—which was moulded from lead. When deposition started, security was ensured by carrying it out in a locked safe, into which the current was led by means of wires passing through the walls, so that the process might continue uninterruptedly during the night.[1] The electrotypes, when deposition was completed, were still only thin shells of copper. In order to give them the required solidity, they were backed with molten solder, which, after it had solidified, was planed down in order to ensure that, when the electrotypes were screwed upon a solid brass block, the 'height to paper'[2] would be correct. The complete note was divided into nine portions, each of which had its separate electrotype, and, as the screw holes in the blocks were uniform, as well as those in the electrotypes themselves, one 'piece' could be changed, if worn or damaged, without impairing the identity of the notes.

On 14 July 1853, after two years' concentration on the development of the process, Hensman and Coe submitted a report to the Court of Directors, together with a specimen note 'produced by electrotypes and printed at the surface press'. In this report, it was pointed out that the new process offered increased security, since the original reliefs were cut from solid metal and the possibility of imitation by the ordinary copper-plate engraver was, therefore, out of the question, as was evidenced by the difficulty

[1] One of the Smee cells used by the Bank is now in the Museum collection at St Luke's Printing Works.
[2] The uniform height of type: in Great Britain it is .9185 of an inch.

that they had experienced in securing engravers who could perform the task. Further, the use of electrotypes produced from moulds of an original relief ensured that the identity of the notes would be preserved, and as the printing was upon dry paper, not only would the delay due to the damping process be avoided, but the notes could be examined and taken into store as soon as they had been printed, instead of waiting until they had been dried and pressed. In addition to these advantages, the cost of production, it was estimated, would be materially reduced. On the same date, the Court of Directors decided to adopt the recommendation, and ordered that the new process should be put into practice at once, with the view to the accumulation, as soon as was practicable, of a sufficient stock of notes to enable all denominations to be issued at the same time.

In order to ensure that the printing should be of the highest standard, considerable attention had been paid to the choice of a machine upon which to carry it out. In 1852, the Bank had purchased two cylinder machines for the purpose, but after considerable trial and experiment it had been decided that the best results would be achieved by the use of a platen press. It may be mentioned that, in the cylinder machine, the paper is held on the periphery of the cylinder and meets, as the cylinder revolves, the forme of type or the relief block, already inked by the movement backwards and forwards beneath the inking rollers of the flat bed to which it is fixed. The platen press, on the other hand, was a mechanical version of the old hand press, where the paper, held in position on a sheet of vellum, known as the tympan, by a parchment framework—the frisket—was inserted beneath the platen which then descended vertically and exerted the necessary pressure so that the paper received the impression from the

H

face of the forme of type or the relief block, previously inked by having been 'rolled-up' by hand. In the mechanical platen press, the inking was effected in the same manner as has been described for the cylinder press.

The press chosen was an improved version of the Napier platen press, which had been patented in 1853 by J. M. Napier[1] of D. Napier & Son, a firm which, besides being famed for their precision machinery—they had made William Cotton's gold-weighing machine[2]—were at that time one of the leading manufacturers of printing machinery. As may be seen from Plate XIII, the press was operated from both ends, at each of which were stationed two boys,[3] one to lay on the paper and the other to take off the printed notes. The paper was laid to points on to a tympan which carried it beneath the platen, and after printing returned it to the same end, where it was taken off and stacked in a wooden trough, from which it was collected by the security staff.[4] While the sheet which had been laid on at one end of the machine was being printed, the boy at the other end laid on a sheet, and the operation was repeated at that end. This alterna-

[1] J. M. Napier was the son of David Napier, who had come from Leith in 1808 to be a pupil of Henry Maudslay, whose works formed, as it were, a university for the young engineers of the period. He came of a family of brilliant engineers, who, it has been said, were descendants of John Napier, the Laird of Merchiston and the inventor in the early seventeenth century of logarithms and of the first calculating device, known as 'Napier's Bones'. The firm, which will be remembered as the producers of the Napier motor-car and of the Lion aeroplane engine, is still actively engaged in engineering.   [2] See p. 94 n.

[3] Boys had first been employed by the printing department in 1847 to operate a paging machine invented by Thomas Oldham, but this occasion was the first upon which they were employed on the printing of bank-notes.

[4] The output of one end of the machine was referred to as an 'end' of notes, an expression which continued in use for more than ninety years, long after the printing of bank-notes by this double-ended machine had ceased.

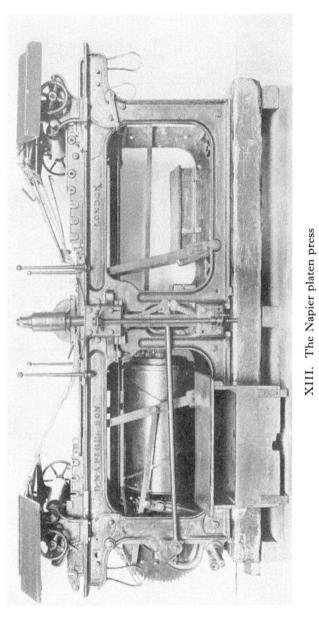

XIII. The Napier platen press

tion, whereby the time occupied in laying on paper was utilised for printing, enabled the machine to achieve a high output for a platen press, namely 750 impressions (1500 notes) per hour from each end of the machine. But the outstanding feature of the machine—it was, in fact, the subject matter of the patent—was the inking device, by which the relief block was inked, not only as it passed under the stationary rollers, but also at a moment when it was at rest—before the descent of the platen—when the rollers themselves moved over it. By this means, the block was inked four times by each of the rollers, with which the machine was equipped, the equivalent, according to Dr Smee, of having been inked twenty times by the old hand-operated roller.

One of the first problems that had emerged from the early experiments in the new method had been the difficulty of producing on the hard bank-note paper, 'fine' printing which would bear comparison with an impression from an engraved plate. It will be remembered that the pressure exerted by a surface printing press is firm but slight—the type is, in fact, said only to 'kiss' the paper—and, if too great a pressure is used, the impression, though clear, is sunk into the paper by the excessive pressure of the type. The problem of how to use the maximum pressure without incurring this disadvantage was solved by the use of a special 'overlay', a device, which in its simplest form consists in the pasting of successive pieces of paper upon the tympan or the impression cylinder, as the case may be, at places where a greater pressure is required, a process known as 'making ready'. The overlay that was used for the printing of the bank-notes was, however, a much more elaborate affair. It was not 'patched up' on the tympan, but was made separately of six pieces of moderately thick paper, each bearing an impression, one of which was used as a master sheet. From the remaining five sheets, certain portions of the print were cut out and pasted on to the master, thereby producing a note, as it were built up in relief, which was fixed to the tympan at the exact place where the impression would be printed. Thus, each note had this hard backing behind every line to be printed, permitting the use of considerable pressure, which, without the overlay, would have resulted, more especially where the lines were fine, in the print appearing in a deep valley. The elaborate nature of these overlays made them expensive in the matter of labour, for the cutting of overlays for one plate, that is to say two notes, employed one skilled craftsman for 137 hours.[1] But the use of this overlay together with the superb inking and the equable pressure of the platen press, was to produce a note which astonished the experts that so perfect a result could have been attained by surface printing.

While electrician, engineer and printer, in happy collaboration, were laying their plans to ensure that the printing should be of the highest standard, no less attention was being given to the production of the paper. As soon as the Bank had in 1851 acquired the patent rights in Brewer and Smith's invention, John Smith had moved his business into the Bank, just as George Cole had brought in his printing business in 1791, and until they were absorbed into the staff of the Bank in 1877, the Smith family[2] carried on their craft, again like the Coles, as a separate

[1] This practice continued until 1937, when chalk overlays were taken into use. These overlays were made by pulling an impression on special paper, surfaced with chalk, which readily dissolved where it was unprinted, leaving the printed lines in relief, a process which took rather less than half an hour.

[2] The manufacture of watermark plates remained in the Smith family for three generations until the retirement in 1940 of F. A. Smith, the grandson of John Smith.

firm, being paid by the piece for the watermark plates that they produced. In 1851, too, it was arranged that the moulds should be made by the Brewers—Charles Brewer had now joined the firm—at Laverstoke, where they were taken over by Wyndham Portal, who had succeeded his father—John Portal had died in 1848—and who then engaged in the trials and experiments that led to the production of a very perfect paper. The preliminary work at the Bank and at Laverstoke was carried out with such speed and efficiency that, in less than eighteen months from the order to proceed, an adequate stock of new notes had been built up, so that, on 22 December 1854, the Bank were able to insert in the *London Gazette* a notification to the effect that all notes dated 1 January 1855 and after, would be of a new pattern, particulars of which were given.

Let us then look at one of these notes as it was first seen by the public in January 1855. The vignette had been the first item to be dealt with, and in 1850 Daniel Maclise, Royal Academician, and one of the leading painters of the day, had at the Bank's request designed a new one, in respect of which he had received a fee of £100. There is no need to describe the vignette, for one has only to look at any present-day Bank of England note to see a reproduction of Robinson's engraving of Maclise's delightful work, which, having regard to the annual output of Bank of England notes, and to the fact that since 1855 this vignette has appeared on every one of them, must, it is thought, make it the most frequently reproduced design ever known. It will be seen that, in his treatment of the figure, Maclise adhered to tradition and delineated the Bank's own Britannia, seated, bareheaded, and armed with a spear, unlike the figure on the coinage which had acquired a number of attributes unknown to John Roettier's Britannia. In 1797, for example, the spear had been replaced by a trident, presumably because Britannia, both in song and in fact, was 'ruling the waves' to some effect at that time, and it was therefore deemed fitting to arm her with the weapon of the old sea god, while in 1821 the figure had acquired a helmet, possibly because Pistrucci required it for the composition of his design. It was fitting, therefore, that Maclise eschewed these innovations, and reproduced in his vignette the original figure, the attributes of which, throughout the Bank's history, have remained unaltered.

Another important change was the abandonment of the practice which had for long ceased to have any real significance, of inserting the name of the Bank's Chief Cashier as payee, and the notes were now payable 'to Bearer', with no named payee.[1] The signature was still that of one of the Bank's cashiers, although it was now printed instead of being written by hand, an innovation which had been made in 1853. A recommendation that the signatures of notes should be printed in conjunction with the numbering and dating was, in fact, one of the last proposals made by Thomas Oldham, and had been adopted by the Bank after an Act of Parliament had been passed to authorise the practice. Incidentally, this Act would appear to have been unnecessary, for, as we know, the printing of the signatures of bank-notes had been authorised by an Act of 1820. As for the paper, here too there is no need to describe it, for by holding to the light a present-day £5 note, there will be seen, with one small difference, the patent watermark of William Brewer and John Smith, which the public saw for the first time in 1855. The difference referred to consisted of the inclusion in the watermark,

---

[1] The omission of the name of the Chief Cashier necessitated a rearrangement of the text, the first line of which now reads 'I promise to pay the Bearer on Demand'.

just below the word 'FIVE', of a reproduction of the signature of the Chief Cashier 'M. MARSHALL', on the assump-
tion, perhaps, that the public, having become accustomed
to seeing his name as payee on every Bank of England
note for the previous twenty years,[1] might regard it as
evidence of authenticity. In short, with the exception of
a few slight differences, both paper and printing were the
same as those of the £5 note of today.

[1] Matthew Marshall had been appointed Chief Cashier in 1835.

CHAPTER VI

FROM 1855 TO THE FIRST WORLD WAR

THE ISSUE of the new notes was marked at the
Bank by the award of gratuities to the officials and
members of the staff of the printing department,
whose ingenuity and persistence had made it possible, and
at the same time pensions and appropriate compensation
were granted to the engravers and plate-printers, whose
services were no longer required. There is no evidence
that the general public exhibited any great interest in the
new note, but *The Times* commented upon it in the following terms. 'Its appearance, at a hasty glance, is very little
different from that of the old Note, although upon examination its superiority is very striking, both as regards clear-
ness of execution of the design and the watermark of the
paper.' Perhaps the general public had taken no more than
a hasty glance.

The change in the method of printing was, however, of
the greatest interest to one section of the community,
namely the bank-note engravers and printers, whose
opinion was voiced by Henry Bradbury in a lecture delivered to the Royal Institution in 1856. Bradbury's
lecture was a detailed criticism of the use of surface printing for the production of security documents such as bank-
notes. He enlarged upon the superiority of plate-printing
and in support of his strong advocacy of ornamental
machine engraving, produced as exhibits two machines
recently invented and constructed by F. J. Wagner of
Berlin, one for medallion engraving, the other being an

improved form of the rose engine. He illustrated his own idea of what a bank-note should be by the exhibition of specimen notes, designed by his friend John Leighton. These trial notes, although beautifully plate-printed by Bradbury and Evans, were not imposing in so far as the designs and the vignettes were concerned, and a study of these features in comparison with those of the Bank of England note provides no justification for Bradbury's criticism that Maclise's vignette 'was alike deficient in conception and execution' or that the note itself was 'unworthy of the Bank and of the Nation'. During his lecture, Bradbury quoted extensively from the observations of Mr Grubb, the engineer of the Bank of Ireland, where, doubtless, the Oldham tradition still held sway. Grubb was severely critical of 'Mr Smee's method', and deplored the lack of security in the new note, which, he suggested, would now depend solely upon the use of 'a highly expensive paper'. There was, as we know, much to be said in favour of plate-printing, but, on studying the criticisms that were directed against the Bank's new production, one cannot but feel that much of it would have been equally applicable to the very methods that the critics themselves recommended. In one respect, however, Bradbury made a very valuable contribution to the study of bank-note protection, when, in the course of his lecture, he drew attention to the dangers of photography in facilitating forgery.

Since the early experiments of Niepce and Daguerre in France, and the work of Fox Talbot in this country, the art of photography had become well known, more particularly as a means of producing portraits. The studios of its practitioners were visited, not only by those who could not afford to employ a portrait painter, and to whom photography was the only method of obtaining a portrait of themselves or of their relatives, but also by the wealthy, who were curious to explore the possibilities of the new invention. There was no thought that the new process could, in any way, be utilised for the forgery of banknotes, until in 1845 Antoine Claudet, who had been a partner of Daguerre, and who had set up in this country as a portrait photographer, conceived the idea that it might be so used, with the result that he set to work and produced a facsimile of a Bank of England note, in which not only the design but also the watermark were faithfully reproduced. The copy was a photographic silver print, which could in no way deceive even the most unobservant, and the watermark did not, of course, respond on being held up to the light. Claudet took one of his prints to Matthew Marshall, the Chief Cashier of the Bank, and, while admitting that in its present state photography did not constitute a real danger, the possibility that improvments might make it so had led him to think of a method of preventing its use for the purposes of forgery. As is well known, the colours at the red end of the spectrum appear black in a photographic print, while the colours at the other end are to all intents and purposes invisible. Claudet's idea was to introduce into the designs of banknotes a selection of colours which would prevent their effective reproduction by means of the camera, thereby destroying by means of this aspect of photography the very danger that photography itself had created.

Bradbury had taken up Claudet's idea from the printer's point of view, and exhibited at his lecture a specimen of a note, the face of which bore an underprinting in a light tint of red, which would, on being photographed, appear as black and inextricably mixed with the main design. Nobody at that time—except perhaps Fox Talbot—had thought of the possibility of making printing plates by means of photography, and it was not until 1872 that

Gillot produced the first zinc relief block by entirely photographic means. Tribute must, therefore, be paid to Henry Bradbury's foresight in producing, in 1856, this means of confounding the forger, a means which developed side by side with the advance of photography, and is still in world-wide use. The Bank of England note, however, remained unchanged. The quality of the paper and the superb watermark were its safeguard, and remain so to this day. It was all the more disconcerting, therefore, when in 1862 a quantity of bank-note paper was stolen from Laverstoke Mill. Nothing could be done, pending the discovery of the criminals, except to warn the public of the existence of this genuine paper in the wrong hands and urge them to examine more closely the printing of the notes, the quality of which could not be equalled by the forger.

The production of bank-notes by means of surface printing was, at this time, practised not only by the Bank of England, but also by the Banks of France, Belgium and Russia, and in 1860 when the newly formed Government of India decided to issue a Government currency note, which would circulate side by side with the already existing notes of the banks of the three Presidencies, Bengal, Madras and Bombay, it was decided to use this process, and the Secretary of State for India approached the Bank with a proposal that they should undertake the printing. The whole issue was to be no more than four crores (40,000,000) of rupees, so that once the initial stock had been built up, the annual demand would not be great. The Bank agreed to the proposal, and it was arranged that the printing should be carried out on the Napier platen machines, already in use for printing the Bank's own notes. The issue was to consist of notes for Rs. 10, Rs. 20, Rs. 50, Rs. 100, Rs. 500 and Rs. 1000, a proposal that notes for Rs. 5 should be issued having been abandoned on the grounds that the native population who dealt with smaller sums would be more content to receive their wages and the like in the form of the silver rupee to which they were accustomed. The first delivery of notes, which were almost the same size as those of the Bank of England, was made in 1861. They were printed upon Portal's paper, the light-and-shade watermark of which followed the plan of that of the Bank, and included in the design the facsimile signatures of Lord Canning, the Governor General, and of James Wilson, the Financial Member of the Council. The printing also followed the plan of the Bank of England note. The words 'Government of India' were printed in bold letters across the head of the note; a vignette of Queen Victoria appeared in the top dexter corner, and panels on each side of the note showed the amount in words and figures in two native languages, which varied in accordance with the office of issue and the Presidency in which the notes would circulate. The notes were numbered and dated in the same manner as those of the Bank of England, but were not signed, that process being carried out after their arrival in India.

The issue was well received, but as might be expected, the notes came in for some criticism. The paper, for example, was admitted to be tough and of excellent quality, but some controversy arose as to whether it was sufficiently stout to stand the strain of repeated reissue and constant handling by the native population, to say nothing of the weather conditions prevalent during the period of the monsoon. Furthermore, instances were arising of alteration and forgery. In 1864 the Bank engaged in consultation with the India Office and Wyndham Portal on the subject, with the result that in 1867 notes of an entirely new design were issued, including a further denomination for Rs.

10,000. The paper for this issue was slightly stouter; the signatures embodied in the watermark were discontinued and
the note no longer bore a vignette. Protective devices were
introduced in the shape of ornamental panels, and a light
green undertint across the middle of the note denoting the
denomination. The native languages, showing the denominations in words and figures, were now increased to four,
from which it may be supposed that the notes were circu-
lating in a wider area. In 1902 notes for Rs. 5 were
introduced. In 1905 an alteration in the appearance of the
notes for Rs. 5, Rs. 10 and Rs. 50 was made by changing
the colour of the underprint from green to red, and at the
same time the number of the native languages shown upon
the notes was again increased. In 1925 a new form for the
notes of Rs. 5 and Rs. 10 was adopted, but otherwise the
design of the issue of 1867 remained unchanged until the
Government of India took over the printing of their own
currency notes in 1928.

In 1860, an improvement connected with the Bank of
England note paper was introduced. From the earliest
years, a great deal of time and trouble had been constantly
expended in making certain that, before printing, each
sheet of paper was the right side up and the right way
round, in order to ensure that notes were printed neither
on the wrong side of the paper nor upside-down in relation
to the watermark. Each sheet was examined, for this purpose, at the mill when the reams were made up after the
paper had been finally dried and pressed, and at the Bank
the greatest care was exercised in order to ensure that no
sheet was reversed during the process of counting. The
elimination of this labour was achieved by introducing
into the mould a very simple means of marking each sheet
of paper so that a glance at a ream was all that was necessary. The distinguishing marks were made on the sinister

edge of each sheet; the paper for the £5 notes had a flattened corner and those of £10, £20 and £50[1] had small semicircular notches in the same edge in different positions for each denomination. It will be perceived, therefore, that as a sheet was, after printing, cut into two notes, only one half of the notes of the denominations concerned would bear the appropriate mark, a circumstance which would have possessed a slight security value if it were recognised by the public that a note, the sinister edge of which was deckle edged, would show the appropriate marking, whereas a note of which that edge was clean cut would not. In 1865, another change, this time in the watermark of the paper, took place. In the previous year, Matthew Marshall had retired from the service of the Bank, after having held the appointment of Chief Cashier for nearly thirty years, and the facsimile of his signature was accordingly removed from the watermark of the bank-note paper into which it had been introduced in 1855, but that of William Miller, who succeeded him, was not inserted in its place. It may have been that the Bank were already considering a change which was not actually made until a few years later when, in the place of the printed signature of one of the appointed cashiers, that of George Forbes, who was then Chief Cashier, appeared with the words 'Chief Cashier' printed below it. The first note to bear this signature appeared in 1870, and since that date the signature of the Chief Cashier for the time being has appeared, on every Bank of England note, as the official who signs his promise to pay 'on Behalf of the Govr. and Compa.'

Although, as far as the actual printing was concerned,

[1] The notes for £30 and £40 had been discontinued in 1852 and 1851 respectively. The notes for higher sums, printed on paper, the watermark of which showed no denomination, remained unmarked.

the Napier platens took in their stride the production of the notes for the Government of India, the advent of these notes had brought about a definite increase in the work of the Printing Office. A great deal of other work, too, had been taken over by the department, and changes in the constitution had taken place, more especially in the matter of security. In 1853, when the signatures of the notes were first printed, a number of cashiers, who had hitherto spent their time in signing the notes, were no longer required for that purpose, and it was decided to abolish the 'Storekeeper's Office for Bank Note Paper', which had been established in 1810, and to transfer the work to a new office to be known as the 'Cashier's Store'. This office, which was manned by the otherwise redundant cashiers, took over the responsibility of safeguarding the paper and the notes, printed or partly printed, as well as all plates and blocks of a security nature.

As for the Printing Office, although we have seen that from time to time it had undergone changes of name— John Coe was now the 'Superintendent of the Bank Note and General Printing, Numbering and Dating Office'— its composition was still much the same, except that it had acquired a largely increased staff, in order to cope with the new tasks that it was constantly called upon to perform. Dividend warrants, certificates of inscription and all documents of a security nature connected with the Bank Stock and other 'Funds' administered by the Bank had always been produced by the Bank's printers, but the forms and books required for the Bank's work had been obtained from the official stationer and from commercial printers. Gradually, however, the production of these essential supplies had been taken over by the Printing Office, where in 1870 seven separate sections were engaged in active production, namely bank-note printing; bank-note numbering, dating and signing; general printing; ruling; sewing; binding; and warehouse. Three years later, an additional section was set up, the staff of which consisted of one man, a lithographer, and from that time stock certificates and other documents, previously plate-printed, were produced lithographically. The total number of persons employed was more than a hundred, four women sewers, some fifty journeymen of various trades, as well as a number of less skilled workers, and fifty boys. The large number of boys who were employed attracts attention, and it will be of interest to study the development of this branch of the service since an almost negligible few were first engaged in 1847.

The boys were recruited from the sons of Bank messengers and porters, or by recommendation from other members of the staff, and at that time entered the service at the age of ten years. It was realised from the first that their employment offered no prospect of advancement, and the Bank, with a view to safeguarding their future, had set on foot a scheme whereby, as they reached a suitable age, those who were so minded were apprenticed 'to appropriate masters who shall undertake to teach them their various trades according to the custom of such trades', the necessary premiums being paid by the Bank from a fund instituted for that purpose. They were allowed a free choice in this matter, and a variety of trades were selected, but a large number chose to follow the one with which they had been associated, and were apprenticed to printers. Many of these returned to the Bank in due course to carry on their crafts in the Printing Office, where were also employed some of their fellows, who, unable to take advantage of the offer of apprenticeship, had remained in the service of the Bank to find employment as book-keepers and the like in such sections as the warehouse, or as posters,

prickers and stampers in the Bank Note Office.[1] During
their years as boys, they formed a lively, albeit inky, community amid the solemn environment of the Bank. But
they were a very happy community, into which, after
undergoing an exacting initiation ceremony, the newcomer
would be admitted as a 'freeman'. Out of their working
hours, they inhabited the 'Boys' Kitchen', where they
were kept in order by a stern disciplinarian, and in which
they would consume the midday meal that fond mothers
had carefully packed for them, but up to the age of sixteen,
they were not admitted to the enjoyment of the several
canteens that had been set up in that quarter of the Bank
in order that the constant need for beer, characteristic of
the workers of the period, might be met.

Since Lord Althorp's Act of 1833, successive measures
had been enacted to regulate the employment of 'children'
and 'young persons' in factories, and to ensure that their
working hours allowed opportunity for part-time education, which was at that time supplied by voluntary organisations such as the National Society and the British and
Foreign School Society. The Factory Act of 1867 and the
Workshops Act of the same year had extended the
educational aspect of the earlier enactments, but the
Education Act of 1870, which provided for the compulsory
full-time education of 'children' in the Board Schools set
up by the Act, necessitated a change in the conditions of
employment of the Bank's machine boys. A number of
boys of less than thirteen years of age had to be released,
with the exception of ten who were shortly to reach that
age and the status of 'young persons'. These were allowed

[1] The posters, prickers and stampers performed, as it were, the last
rites in the life of a bank-note by stamping it with an identifying number, and marking off in the books of the Bank the date upon which it
had been paid.

I

to remain in their employment, but it was laid down as a condition of this dispensation that the Bank should be responsible for their part-time education until they attained the age of thirteen years. This responsibilty was delegated to the Superintendent of the Printing Office, who thus found himself engaged in an entirely new activity, namely, to arrange for the education of the boys concerned in a manner that would be acceptable to the educational authority.

But the Superintendent of the Printing Office was to become accustomed to responsibilities entirely unconnected with printing. In 1851, for example, when an artesian well had been sunk in a courtyard of the Bank, thereafter known as the Well Yard, the care of this installation had been handed over to the Superintendent of the Printing Office, presumably because the pumping apparatus was driven by his steam engine. In 1875 the post of storekeeper, instituted in 1792, was abolished, and the work of his office was given into the charge of the Superintendent of the Printing Office, who thus became responsible for the custody of the stores of writing paper, pens, ink, sealing-wax, etc., and for the dispensing of these essentials to the clerical staff of the Bank. In 1877, too, on the retirement of Henry Hensman, who had held the appointment of engineer for twenty-six years, no successor was appointed, the duties being added to those of the superintendent of what had now become the 'Printing, Stationery and Storekeeper's' office. But in addition to engineering ability, the superintendent had also to possess a certain amount of architectural knowledge in order that he should not have to meet the Bank's architect on too unequal terms at consultations on the subject of the adaptation of premises required to meet the constant expansion of his department. The actual structural work was under the control of the building committee, and the necessary materials were ordered by the works department, but the responsibility for ordering the remainder of the Bank's day-to-day requirements, such as coal, oil, wood and house requisites, to say nothing of the large quantities of beer required to supply the canteens, had, for some reason, fallen to the Superintendent of the Printing Office, who bade fair to become, as he was referred to in an official memorandum of a few years later, the 'Servant of the whole House'.

In 1880, John Coe retired from the service, and his son, W. J. Coe, who had been Assistant Superintendent since 1876 took his place, with Henry McPherson as his deputy. Henry McPherson, who was then in the forty-third year of his service, was a skilled engineer and endowed with a remarkably inventive mind. In 1869, when he had occupied the position of overseer, he had invented and introduced a new method of printing the dividend books[1] and at the time of his appointment as Deputy Superintendent he was engaged in planning a new machine which was to revolutionise the printing of dividend warrants, but his most valuable contribution to the work of the Bank was his bank-note printing and numbering machine, which in 1881 superseded the Napier platen, and by which the Bank of England notes were printed from that date until 1945. The numbering and dating of notes, ever since these features were first printed in 1809, had always been a separate process, and one of the outstanding qualities of the new machine was the fact that it printed both the main design of the notes and the numbers and dates in one

---

[1] Dividend books are lists of the proprietors of each stock, with the amounts of their holdings, the interest thereon, the tax, and the net amount of the dividend, which are printed in preparation for the payment of dividends.

operation, at a speed which produced 3000 completed notes in an hour, the time previously taken to print only the main design. The first machine, which was ordered in 1880, was built by one of the leading precision engineers, R. W. Munro,[1] of the King's Cross Road, and started printing in 1881. Subsequently, eleven further machines were acquired, and it is of interest to note that, while the cost of the first machine was £750, that of the last to be purchased, in 1917, was £1050.

As will be seen from Plate XIV, the machine was equipped with two large impression cylinders and an intermediate cylinder between them. The two plates upon which the electrotypes were mounted, one to print the main design and the other the numbers and dates, were fixed to a flat table below the cylinders and moved backwards and forwards beneath the inking rollers. The 'date plate', as it was called, bore the dates and the ciphers and was cut away to permit the operation of the numbering wheels, which were made of steel, four inches in diameter, and were mounted on a special spindle. Caslon's beautiful figures, from which the numbers were printed, were cast in type metal and fitted into slots on the periphery of the wheels, where they remained in place solely by the precision of their fitting, so that any figure could be replaced as soon as it showed signs of wear. When the machine was ready to print, a sheet of paper was laid on by a machine boy against the guides, which then moved forward to carry the sheet by means of tapes on to the first cylinder. As the cylinders revolved, the sheet was carried down to the first plate which printed the main design, then up and around

---

[1] R. W. Munro was descended from a long line of precision engineers. The firm, now R. W. Munro Ltd. of New Southgate, still supply the Bank of England with precision machinery, in which branch of engineering they continue to specialise.

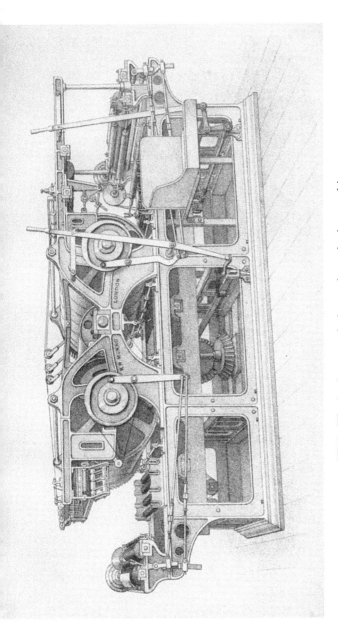

XIV. The bank-note printing and numbering machine

the intermediate cylinder, and down to the other impression cylinder to the second plate, which printed the date and the numbers while the next sheet was being printed by the main plate. The completely printed sheet was then delivered, face upwards, on to a silk band, which conveyed it to a desk where it was inspected by an 'examiner', and as a ream was completed, it was handed over to the security staff for checking. Each machine was equipped with a dial which recorded the number of impressions printed by the first plate (printing the main design) and at the end of the day this record was agreed with the number of notes produced, allowance being made for trial impressions printed upon plain paper. It will be appreciated that, as the notes were delivered face upwards, the sequence of the numbering was necessarily backwards, and in view of the fact that 100,000 notes of the same date, which had to be delivered to the cashiers in proper order, could not be completed on one machine in one day, a system was in use whereby they were numbered in 'set-ups' of ten reams at a time. Thus, the first 'set-up' would be for 10,000 notes—two on each sheet —to be numbered 5000 to 1 and 10,000 to 5001; the next 'set-up' for 15,000 to 10,001 and 20,000 to 15,001, and so on.

The numbering mechanism was a beautiful piece of engineering. As the table reached the extreme end of the machine, an arm was actuated by a cam, setting in motion a ratchet which turned the 'units' wheel. When this wheel had made one complete revolution, a projection which emerged from it engaged with the 'tens' wheel and turned it one-tenth of a revolution. Similarly, the 'tens' wheel turned the 'hundreds', the 'hundreds' the 'thousands' and so on. As each numbering unit consisted of only five wheels, the highest figure that could be printed was 99,999, and the number 100,000 had therefore to be produced by stamping by hand the figure '1' in front of the machine-printed 'oo,ooo'. The result was sometimes, but not always satisfactory, and in order that no imperfect piece of printing should appear in public, the notes numbered 100,000, after they had been delivered to the cashiers, were cancelled before issue, and an appropriate entry made in the books. The fact that the numbers were overprinted upon the words 'I promise 'and 'Demand',[1] made it necessary that the register of the two printings should be as near perfection as possible. The machines had no 'grippers', and the sheets were carried through both processes solely by the tapes, which, in order that the registration should not suffer, had to be kept constantly taut. For the whole of their long life, these machines functioned faultlessly. For sixty-five years, they produced the Bank of England notes, and for forty-seven of them the currency notes for the Government of India, as perfectly as on the first day of their running.

In 1880, an Act of Parliament was passed by which the issue of postal orders was authorised, and the Postmaster-General approached the Bank with a view to their undertaking the manufacture. The Bank agreed to carry out the printing; the requirements of the Post Office were ascertained, and, as soon as the necessary paper was available, printing started. It is not known upon which of the Bank's machines the first issues were printed, but in 1884 R. W. Munro built a rotary machine[2] to the design of Henry McPherson, by which the orders were printed and numbered, eight on a sheet. There were ten denominations, between 1s. and 20s.; the text was printed in the same shade of blue that is still in use for the postal orders of less than ten shillings in value, and the amount was in

[1] See p. 106 n.

[2] In a rotary machine, the printing blocks or plates are curved, and fixed to the periphery of a cylinder, which as it revolves brings them into contact with the paper.

the same bold black figures that are in use today. From time to time, intermediate denominations were introduced; in 1903, postal orders for sixpence and 21*s.* first appeared, and, in 1905, a range of values at intervals of sixpence between that amount and 20*s.* was issued, each one showing the denomination in the watermark.[1]

The orders were at first printed upon hand-made paper, but in 1885 a Fourdrinier paper-making machine was installed at the mill, and issues subsequent to that year were printed upon machine-made paper. Now Bank of England notes have never been printed upon machine-made paper, but a development of this process was in later years used extensively for the production of paper for bank-notes and other security documents, so that it may be of interest to glance briefly at the manner in which the Fourdrinier machine operates. For the mould there is substituted an endless wove-wire band, forty to fifty feet long, which is edged on each side by endless straps of indiarubber to serve as deckles. The pulp, which contains a proportion of vegetable resin to render subsequent sizing unnecessary,[2] is spread evenly upon the wire band at what is known as the 'wet end' of the machine, and travels with it, draining, at first naturally and then by passing over suction boxes and between felted rollers, until it has acquired sufficient consistency to leave the wire band. The web of paper then passes over heated cylinders until it reaches the 'dry end' of the machine as finished paper. The first machine-made paper bore no watermark, but the invention of the 'dandy roll', which impressed a design on to the surface of the paper while it was still sufficiently

[1] Forty-one separate denominations were therefore printed. Since 1939 this number has been reduced to twenty-seven.

[2] The resin is mixed intimately with the pulp in the beating engine, and the process is, therefore, known as 'engine-sizing'.

yielding to receive it, remedied the deficiency, although the resultant watermark was by no means as clear as that of hand-made paper.

Interior lighting by electricity was in a very early stage of its development—the carbon filament lamp that made it possible had been invented only a few years before— when, in 1883, the Bank decided to try the new method for the illumination of the Private Drawing Office.[1] The plant was installed by the Electrical Power Storage Company, who supplied the dynamos and accumulators, and entered into an agreement to maintain the installation for a period of five years. The motive power, however, was provided by the steam engine that drove the machines of the Printing Office, who were thus brought early into contact with the new idea, and who, when the maintenance contract terminated, took over the responsibility for the Bank's electric lighting. The experiment in the Private Drawing Office having been a success, it was decided in 1887 to extend this form of lighting to the court room, the committee rooms and certain favoured offices. In the following year, the scheme was again extended; additional dynamos were acquired, and an electric lighting section was formed from the staff of the Printing Office, which was augmented for that purpose. By 1893, however, the extension of electric lighting had reached a point that taxed to the limit the capacity of the Bank's installation, and arrangements were made to obtain current from the recently formed City of London Electric Lighting Company. But wiring, maintenance and the like were still carried out by the Bank's electric lighting section, and the Superin-

[1] The Private Drawing Office, where the accounts of private individuals and firms were kept, was, in 1933, amalgamated with the Public Drawing Office, in which were kept the accounts of government departments and other public bodies, to form the present-day Drawing Office.

tendent of the Printing Office, who had assumed responsibility for this work as he had for so many other activities
of the Bank entirely unconnected with printing, remained
in charge of the whole of the Bank's electrical arrangements
for as long as the Printing Office remained within the walls
of the Bank.

In *The Bank of England from Within*, Marston Acres
wrote, 'It would not be easy to determine exactly at what
period the Bank of England began to be considered one of
the "sights" of London.' We know, however, that in the
latter part of the last century the Bank was indeed one of
the 'sights'. Visitors, who were frequent and numerous,
were conducted on an organised tour of those activities of
the Bank that were deemed to have an 'entertainment
value', and not the least popular of these activities was the
printing of bank-notes, the prohibition of visitors to the
Printing Office, laid down in 1820, having apparently been
allowed to lapse. The parties of visitors were ushered along
a passage on one side of the bank-note printing room, from
whence they inspected the machines, which were ranged
along the other side of the room, against a row of windows
overlooking the Well Yard. The printing process never
failed to arouse the interest of these spectators, who, it
would appear, were prone on occasion to exhibit too great
an interest, for it was found necessary to equip the machines
with a small framed notice, upon which was printed
'Visitors are requested not to touch the Notes'. Time
passed; the Printing Office moved to St Luke's, and the
most stringent prohibition of visitors was again enforced,
but until the bank-note machines finally ceased to function
in 1945, one of them still exhibited a copy of this notice,
as a relic of the days when the printing of Bank of England
notes was one of the 'sights' of London.

It is a characteristic of visitors to ask questions, and one of these questions is, even today when visitors to the Printing Works are a thing of the past, frequently made the subject of letters from interested inquirers, who seek confirmation of a rumour which they have heard to the effect that, at one time in its history, the Bank printed and issued notes for as small an amount as 1*d*. and for as great as £1,000,000. The answer is, of course, that at no time has the Bank printed or issued such notes, but nevertheless examples of notes of both these denominations exist in the Bank's collection. The explanation of this apparent contradiction lies in the fact that the above-mentioned denominations were not printed, nor were the notes ever issued. There is only one example of a note for 1*d*., a relic of the time when it was a common practice to make use, for internal purposes, of notes for quite small sums, presumably for the adjustment of an overnight difference, for they were always 'cleared' on the following day. The existing example is dated the 10 January 1828, and is written on a £5 note form, the denomination having been altered in manuscript. From the earliest days, all cancelled notes have, after being kept for reference for a number of years, been destroyed by burning, and it can only be thought that this note must have been wrongfully abstracted, and kept as a souvenir, when, together with other notes of the same date, it should have been destroyed. Forty years later, in 1868, it reappeared in the possession of the landlord of the 'Blue Last' in Bell Alley, who would show it to his customers as a curiosity. It was felt, no doubt, that such a document would be better in the possession of the Bank than in that of the 'Blue Last', and it was, accordingly, purchased for the sum of £1 and placed in the Bank's note collection.

There are two existing examples of notes for £1,000,000 and eleven of £500,000, of various dates up to 1812. These notes, too, were used only for internal transactions, in order to avoid the labour involved in moving large quantities of notes, and were written, with the necessary alterations, on a form of note that had been notified to the public as obsolete. In later years this practice was regularised by the printing of what were known as 'giant' notes for sums of £50,000 and £100,000, which were overprinted in large type with the words 'For internal use only, and not available outside the Bank'.

The manufacture of relief blocks by photographic means, of which we have noted the beginning, had, by the 'eighties of last century, been taken up extensively by commercial interests, and a number of periodicals had adopted this method for the production of their illustrations. The increased facility that this process gave to the forger, foreseen by Alphonse Claudet and Henry Bradbury some thirty years before, had led to the adoption by bank-note printers of the protective colour device suggested by those far-sighted technicians. The bank-note printers had, too, remained faithful to plate printing, aided by the extensive use of machine engraving, while the identity of their notes was maintained by the use of the plate transfer machine.[1] As we have seen, the Bank of Ireland were early in the field in employing these processes, but the Scottish Banks were not slow to follow, and examples of rose-engine work are to be seen on Scottish notes that were issued very soon after the process had become known. The notes of the English and Welsh country banks still retained their resemblance to those of the Bank of England, except that

[1] It is a matter of interest that Perkins & Bacon, as the firm had become after the retirement of Charles Heath, had, in 1840, secured the contract for engraving the first postage stamps, a piece of work which provided a striking example of the utility of the plate transfer machine, since it involved the production of 240 identical engravings on one plate.

most of them had adopted an undertint of protective colouring. But these notes, and in fact all British bank-notes other than those of the Bank of England, bore for some years further evidence of authenticity in the duty stamp embossed upon them in respect of the Revenue Tax.[1] The raising of revenue by means of a tax upon documents of value had been practised for some years, but it was first imposed upon promissory notes payable to bearer on demand in 1791. After the manner of most taxes, it started in a small way, but in 1804 the tax was consolidated, and a graduated scale of stamp duties laid down, from 3*d.* on notes not exceeding one guinea, to 7*s.* 6*d.* on those of £500 to £1000, while notes for any sum greater than £1000 were subjected to a tax of 10*s.* This scale, augmented from time to time, remained in force until 1828, when the country banks were allowed to compound, at a cost of 3*s.* 6*d.* per cent half-yearly, on the average amount of their notes in circulation.

Since that date, however, the issues of the English country banks had gradually declined. The establishment, in 1826, of branches of the Bank of England had provided an alternative to the issues of the local banks, and in 1841 the Bank entered into an agreement with certain country banks, by which the latter would relinquish their right to issue notes and would issue instead Bank of England notes, in consideration of a payment by the Bank of 1 per cent per annum on the average amount of the Bank of England notes issued to them which were still in circulation. This arrangement, again, started in a small way, but by 1844, when it was regularised and the rate of composition fixed by the Bank Charter Act of that year, there were forty-

---

[1] At no time did the Bank of England notes bear a revenue stamp. From the date of the introduction of the tax, the Bank was allowed to compound, until under the provisions of the Bank Charter Act of 1844, Bank of England notes were exempted from tax.

three country banks in receipt of these payments, which, it was enacted, should cease in August 1856. This provision was, however, repealed in June of that year, and the principle of compensation continued. As time went on, too, an increasing number of country banks lost their right of issue on their absorption by the great joint stock banks, who, since they had opened offices in London had lost that right. The issues of country banks grew less and less, and finally ceased in 1921, when Messrs Fox Fowler & Co. of Wellington, the last country bank to issue its own notes, was amalgamated with Lloyds Bank Ltd. The cessation of these issues had affected the Bank's printers, who were in consequence called upon for greater production; it would, too, have been a severe blow to the London firms who specialised in bank-note printing, had it not been that they had entered a much wider field, in which they competed with one another and with the American Bank-Note Company[1] for the work of printing bank-notes for most of the countries of the world.

We have seen that in 1822 the denominations of Bank of England notes for £5 to £50 were first shown in the watermark, and that in 1860 the paper for these denominations was distinguished by an appropriate mark on the edge of each sheet. In 1887 both these devices were extended to the paper for notes of higher sums, £100, £200, £500, and £1000,[2] which thenceforth showed their respective denominations in the watermark, and were distinguished by further notches at intervals on the edge of the paper. Four years later, however, it was not the notes for high sums that occupied the public mind, but those of

[1] The American Bank-Note Company was incorporated in 1851 from a firm which dated from the War of Independence, and had since joined forces with a number of the leading security printers of the United States.

[2] The notes for £300 had been discontinued in 1885.

very much smaller denominations, namely, £1 and 10s. A proposal that such notes should be issued was made by the Chancellor of the Exchequer[1] in an after-dinner speech to the Chamber of Commerce of Leeds in January 1891. He recalled to his hearers the financial crisis that had shaken the country at the end of the preceding year, and in the introduction to his speech he paid tribute to the timely and public-spirited action of the Bank of England, inspired by the leadership of the Governor, in stemming the tide and preventing what would have been nothing less than a catastrophe. But, said the Chancellor, the crisis would never have reached the serious height to which it had risen had there been a larger reserve of gold in the country, and he announced his plan for the enlargement of the gold reserve by the issue of notes for £1 and 10s. 'One bird in the hand', he said, 'is worth two in the bush', and went on to say that he would prefer to have £20,000,000 in his hand rather than '£30,000,000 in the bush, that is to say, in the pockets of the community'. During the succeeding months, the merits and demerits of this proposal formed the subject of discussion and, although the financial aspect of the question is beyond our scope, there was among the objections to the scheme one that we must consider, namely, the danger of forgery.

Although the Bank had ceased to issue notes for £1 and £2 in 1821, they had continued to circulate with forgeries among them for many years after that date. Between 1843 and 1881 £1 and £2 notes to the value of £9304 were paid, so that even in 1891, there were many people who could remember the doubt and uncertainty that had attended the appearance of one of these notes, and the opinion was expressed that the proposed notes might be largely forged.

[1] The Rt Hon. G. J. Goschen, created Viscount Goschen of Hawkhurst in 1900.

But the Chancellor did not attach any great importance to this objection, and in a speech to the London Chamber of Commerce in December of the same year, he explained away the prevalence of the forgery of £1 and £2 notes in the early days of the century. It was, he suggested, the administration that was at fault, in neglecting the detection and prevention of forgery, while relying upon ferocious punishment as a deterrent. This contention was possibly based upon a recollection of Ricardo's criticism of the Bank's efforts to combat the excessive forgery of bank-notes during the period of the restriction, which criticism, as we have already noted, was perhaps ill-founded. The Chancellor was more convincing, however, when he pointed out that it was not only the notes for £1 and £2 that were forged in the early days of the century. The notes for higher sums were also freely forged, and he quoted figures to show how greatly the number of these had declined during the intervening years.[1] Moreover, the crime of counterfeiting the coinage, which had been rife at the same time, had been greatly reduced, and he felt confident that, if £1 notes were again issued—the proposal to issue notes for ten shillings had been abandoned—the same principle would apply.

After the delivery of this second speech, arguments for and against the scheme were again heard. Informed opinion seems to have been divided on the subject, and the Chancellor's next step was awaited with interest. It was surprising, therefore, that, when the next session of Parliament opened in the following February, no indication of Government action was given in the speech from the

[1] The number of forged notes, which had fallen sharply at the cessation of the issue of notes for £1 and £2, had decreased year by year, and continued to decline even after the manufacture of printing blocks by photographic means was in general use.

throne, unless it were a reference to the revision of existing
agreements with the Bank of England, in what was described, during the debate on the address, as 'an obscure
corner' of the gracious speech. The Chancellor was asked
'whether he meant business or not', and when he was going
to tell the House of Commons and the country what he
was going to do about the currency. The Chancellor was,
however, not to be drawn into battle. What may have
occurred behind the political scene is not known, but
neither in the Budget speech in April nor in the speech
with which he introduced the 'Banks of England and Ireland (Payments) Bill' in June was any mention made of
his plan. 'The infant', as a political opponent said in reference to the first mention of the scheme, 'had but a short
and unhealthy life . . . made away with by its own parent.'
Thus it was that the £1 notes proposed in 1891 did not
materialise, and gold in the form of sovereigns and half-
sovereigns, remained 'in the pockets of the community'.

It will be remembered that in 1853, when the Cashiers'
Store was established, the new office was manned by
cashiers who were no longer required for signing the bank-
notes. Since then the original staff, known at first as
supernumerary cashiers and later as sub-cashiers, had, as
they retired, been replaced by clerks of advanced seniority,
and in 1893, when it was decided to reorganise this office,
there were eight of these sub-cashiers who, although they
could perform efficiently their day's work, which consisted
in counting and checking the notes as they came from the
printers, were stated to be 'unfitted for active work'. The
bank-note machines, at that time, ceased printing at
3 o'clock in order that the notes might be lodged in the
Bank's Treasury by 4 p.m., but it was now decided that
they should continue to print until 4 o'clock, the additional
notes being housed for the night in an adequately pro-

tected strong-room, adjacent to the Cashiers' Store. At the same time, the designation 'sub-cashier' was abolished and the eight remaining holders of that title were replaced by three more active clerks, who, it was decided, would be quite capable of dealing with the work, including the counting and checking of the notes that were printed during the additional hour. This reorganisation had left the regulations for the maintenance of security unchanged, but in 1895 it was decided that a further check should be carried out by the Bank's audit department, which had been created in the preceding year. The day-to-day control by the Printing Office and the Cashiers' Store remained as before, but at approximately half-yearly intervals the Bank's auditors would engage in a stock-taking of un-printed paper, in reams, and of printed notes and other securities, in detail, a practice which has been maintained until the present day.

There were no further developments in the history of the Bank of England note during the otherwise notable 'nineties of last century, but in 1903 an addition was made to the form of the notes by the repetition of the cipher and number, printed in small type immediately above the sig-nature. This addition seems to have aroused little interest among the public who daily handled the notes, and few will have speculated upon the reason for its appearance, but the story of how it came about is, it is thought, an interesting one. Every Bank of England note, as it is paid, is cancelled by the method that has been in use from the beginning, namely, by tearing off the corner of the note which bears the signature, and is then posted as 'paid' in the books of the Bank. In order to provide against the possi-bility of the loss or destruction of cancelled notes sent from the branches for this purpose, it had been the practice, ever since 1826, when the first branch was established,

K

to prepare lists, showing the numbers and dates of the notes that were dispatched to the Head Office, so that in the event of loss the necessary posting could be carried out from these particulars, which had been retained at the branch. But in 1872 it was decided to discontinue the preparation of these lists; the notes were stamped on the back with a number that would serve to identify them, and were sent to the head office by a special messenger in order to guard against the possibility of loss. This practice continued until 1897, when the matter was again considered, and it was decided that thenceforth the cancelled notes should be cut in half and sent to the Head Office separately, the halves being subsequently assembled and stuck together. This otherwise excellent idea provided in practice a burdensome task for the staff of the bank-note library in storing for reference bundles of notes, which, as a result of the sticking-together process, were twice as thick in the middle as they were at the edges. But in 1903, the problem was solved by the printing of the third number on all Bank of England notes, the corners of the notes, which were removed on cancellation, and which now bore the number, being kept at the branch until notification had been received from the Head Office that the relative posting had been completed.

In 1905, the driving of the Bank's printing machinery by steam power, which had been regarded as a tremendous advance when it had been introduced in 1836, was discontinued, and individual electric motors were installed for that purpose. In these days, the modern all-electric equipment of workshops and factories is taken very much as a matter of course, as is many another improvement when the system that it replaced has once been forgotten. There are some who have never seen a workshop of the old-fashioned type where all the machinery was steam propelled, but those of us who knew them, not so long ago, will remember the constant clicking of shafting which, running overhead as it usually did, helped to obscure such daylight as might have entered by way of the skylights, and the persistent movement of the belting that descended from the revolving shafts to each machine, to prove a dangerous neighbour in the event of its being deflected or breaking. Now, all these accompaniments of a day's work are things of the past; the turn of a switch, the throwing in of a gear, and the machine is in action. The effect of the substitution of electric motors for steam power upon the health and well-being of all those who worked amid machinery was incalculable, and from the time of their introduction into the Bank, the Printing Office was a happier and healthier place.

Another advantage of electric propulsion lay in the fact that, while the machines were dependent upon steam power, they had to be located within the possible range of the shafting, but now it was a comparatively simple matter to run a cable even to the most remote part of the premises when a new machine was to be erected, a very marked advantage at that time, when additional machinery was frequently required on account of the persistent increase of work in all sections of the Printing Office. The increase of work had led to a corresponding augmentation of the staff, which now consisted of some two hundred employees, while the administrative staff now numbered three, a Principal—the Superintendent had been so renamed in 1901—a Deputy Principal and an assistant. In 1907 W. J. Coe retired after forty-two years' service. During the next four years, a number of appointments of short duration were made until 1912, when H. G. de Fraine became Principal and S. B. Chamberlain Assistant Principal. The Post of Deputy Principal remained vacant, but was filled a few years later by the promotion of Chamberlain, whose place as assistant was filled by J. R. Dudin.

The reorganisation of 1893 had, as we have seen, involved an addition of five hours to the working week of the staff engaged upon bank-note printing, but the hours of the Printing Office were still far behind those of the printing trade in general. In 1912, however, there was a complete review of hours of work; a working week of forty-eight hours was instituted, and time-recording clocks were installed in order to ensure that unpunctuality in arriving at work and excess of punctuality in leaving it might be avoided. It cannot be thought that an increase in the hours of work would be welcomed by the staff, but they had also to take into consideration advantages that they would not enjoy in other employment, namely, non-contributory pensions, holidays with pay, pay during sickness, and the privilege of obtaining inexpensive meals at their mess room, which had been set up by the Bank in 1902 at premises, leased for that purpose in Bow Lane; moreover, the hours to be worked were still less than those of the printing trade in general, and the rate of payment for overtime was higher. The contemplation of this side of the picture was, apparently, decisive, for the adult staff accepted the new terms unanimously. The only opposition that arose was from an entirely unexpected quarter, namely, the machine boys, whose conditions of work were incomparably better than those of the 'printer's devil' of the period, and who, one would have thought, had every reason for showing gratitude towards a benevolent employer. Nevertheless, on 19 September,[1] to the astonishment of

[1] The new terms of employment had not been announced on that date, but the time-recording clocks had been installed only two days before, and, according to the boys' spokesman, had seriously curtailed their meal-time—they also enjoyed the amenities of Bow Lane—on account of the delay occasioned by their checking in and out.

the authorities, the machine boys thought fit to strike. The evening newspapers were not slow to exploit the 'news value' of this incident, and, in a remarkably short time, newsboys were running through the City, shouting after the fashion of the time, and displaying contents bills bearing the words 'STRIKE AT THE BANK OF ENGLAND'. The situation was handled calmly, but firmly, by the officials of the Printing Office. The boys were informed that those who wished to return were free to do so, but out of 114 boys, only 22 remained in the service. There was no lack of recruits, however, and within a few months the staff of boys numbered 100. But it was the beginning of the end of the history of the Bank's machine boys; four years later, this branch of the staff ceased to exist, and, beginning in 1914, girls were employed in their place.

One of the problems that constantly harassed the Principal of the Printing Office was the need of more space in which to operate even as it had harassed Garnet Terry a hundred years before. The Printing Office had encroached upon neighbouring territory to an extent that had led the remainder of the Bank to regard them as land-grabbers of the worst type, and, truth to tell, they had spread, in positively octopus fashion, over much of their quarter of the Bank, of which the old Well Yard formed the centre. In 1912, a very considerable extension took place, when a large basement beneath the Public Drawing Office of those days was allotted to the Printing Office, while other quarters were found for the bank-note library by which it had been occupied. This additional space was used for the printing of postal orders, a branch of the work which had grown enormously.

Starting in quite a small way, the demand for postal orders had increased with the passing of each year, and by 1910 the output had risen to 132 millions per annum.

Further, a demand for particular denominations would, on occasion, suddenly arise. The 'Limerick' competition of 1907, for example, had led to so great a demand for six-penny postal orders, one of which had to accompany each entry, that the output for that year had increased by twenty millions, and similarly other denominations would be in demand in large numbers and at very short notice as the result of some quite unimportant circumstance. The postal orders were still printed on Henry McPherson's machines, to which his son, Alfred McPherson, had made a number of improvements. They now printed and numbered ten orders on a sheet. They printed, also, the regulations on the backs of the orders, and included a perforating device to facilitate the separation of the counterfoils introduced in 1903. The same machines were used for the Old Age Pension orders, the printing of which had been undertaken by the Bank from their introduction in 1908, and for which purpose Alfred McPherson had invented an ingenious dating attachment, there being no date on a postal order. But in 1912 provision was made for 'peak' demands by the installation of a new rotary machine, which printed and numbered a sheet of forty postal orders at a time, and which operated at a very high speed. The machine, which was the only one of its kind, was specially designed and constructed by R. Hoe & Co. Ltd. It was similar to the big machines used for the printing of newspapers, but the precision necessary in order that the forty curved electrotypes might register correctly on the water-marked paper, and the incorporation of eighty automatic numbering units presented problems which, although new to this type of machine, were successfully overcome. The machine was used only for the denominations chiefly in demand, and it served its purpose admirably, but it was to achieve a positive triumph when two years later the war

of 1914 broke out, and by a clause in the Currency and
Bank Notes Act of 6 August, it was enacted that postal
orders were to be legal tender for any amount. As in 1797,
the Bank's printers again came to the rescue, and produced
on this occasion large quantities of postal orders, more
especially those for 20s. and 10s., in order to reinforce the
as yet small supply of the new currency notes authorised
by the same Act, a feat which would have been impossible
had it not been for the Hoe postal order machine.

Although Great Britain did not enter the war until mid-
night on 4/5 August, its approach had been felt during the
preceding week, as, one by one, the nations of Europe were
drawn into the contest. During the latter part of this
week, and throughout the following month, the bank-note
machines worked day and night, producing notes, chiefly
those for £5, in order to augment the existing stocks
against possible demands, while, in the inner sanctuary of
the Printing Office, work was proceeding upon the production of a Bank of England £1 note, which the Bank
had been asked to prepare.

The proposed note was a beautiful piece of work, being
a miniature—$3\frac{13}{16}$ inches by 6 inches—of the notes for
higher sums, the dimensions of which were $5\frac{3}{16}$ inches by
$8\frac{3}{8}$ inches; it was plate-printed, and showed in the top
dexter corner the 'old' vignette of Brittania which had
preceded Maclise's design. The work was accomplished
with the greatest dispatch, but when a proof was submitted
to H.M. Treasury, the Bank were informed that a contract
had already been entered into for the supply of currency
notes by Waterlow Bros. & Layton Ltd. The work was
executed with incredible speed, and on 6 August,[1] a limited

[1] The day upon which the banks reopened, after having been closed
for four days. August bank holiday, which fell upon the 3rd of that
month, had been extended to three days by proclamation.

supply—2½ millions—of currency notes, or, as they were usually called, treasury notes, for £1 were ready for issue. Speed, however, had been attained only at the expense of quality, for the new notes were by no means good examples of printing. The paper used was that upon which the postage stamps were printed, bearing an overall watermark consisting of repetitions of the royal cipher, 'G.R.'; the notes (2½ inches by 5 inches) were surface printed in black, and besides the text, they showed, in a panel on the dexter side, the head of the king. They were signed by Sir John Bradbury, the Permanent Secretary to the Treasury, and were in consequence popularly known as 'Bradburys', a name which persisted even after 1919, when Sir Warren Fisher succeeded Sir John Bradbury as Permanent Secretary. The notes for 10s., which were issued a week later, were of the same size and design, but were printed in red, some by Waterlow Bros. & Layton Ltd. and some by Thomas De La Rue & Co. Ltd.

It was appreciated that there was room for improvement, and a few months later, notes of a new design were issued. The £1 notes, printed by Thomas De La Rue & Co. Ltd., appeared in October 1914, and the 10s. notes, printed as before, by both of the above-mentioned firms, in the following January. The notes of this second series were slightly larger; the dimensions of those for £1 being 3¼ inches by 6 inches, and those for 10s., 3 inches by 5½ inches. The distinguishing colours were the same, but the notes now bore a vignette of the king's head in the top dexter corner, balanced on the sinister side by a representation of St George and the Dragon surrounded by the Garter. In a short time, a sufficient stock of currency notes had been accumulated to enable the Government to dispense with the use of postal orders as currency, and in February 1915, the relative clause in the Act of 1914 was revoked by Proclamation. An interesting feature of the second series of currency notes was that they were printed upon paper with a waved-line watermark. The Bank's proprietary instincts were aroused, and some correspondence with the Government ensued on the subject of this breach of the law. But *quis custodiet ipsos custodes*? No action was taken, and the same paper remained in use until the third series appeared, the £1 notes in 1917 and the 10s. notes in 1918. The new issue was an improvement upon the second series. The size of the notes was unaltered, but the text of the £1 notes was printed in green over a large design, in brown, of St George and the dragon on the dexter side, while on the sinister side was a vignette of the king's head, printed by photogravure,[1] Waterlow Bros. & Layton Ltd. having acquired a large plant at Watford, where this process was carried out. The 10s. notes were similarly printed, except that a figure of Britannia, printed in green, took the place of St George, the text being printed in brown.

Although the Bank's printers had not been called upon to print the notes for small sums, they were, nevertheless, intensively occupied in other directions. In addition to the increased output of postal orders already referred to, the printing of large quantities of postal drafts, Navy, Army, and, later, Air Force drafts, by which allowances were paid to the dependants of serving personnel, constituted a formidable task. The drafts were bound, as were the Old Age Pension orders, in booklets; as the forces concerned increased in number, so did the drafts, the output of which, in a few years' time, amounted to approximately one

[1] Photogravure is effected by photographing the original picture or object through a fine screen, the consequent reticulated negative being printed photographically on to copper and lightly etched in. The subsequent printing process is similar to plate-printing, and produces an effect resembling mezzotint.

million drafts per day, and, at 'peak' periods, when new booklets were to be issued, to as much as three million drafts per day. Conditions in India had led to an increased demand for notes of small denominations; notes for Rs. 5 were required in large quantities, and it became necessary to design and to prepare proofs for notes of Rs. 1 and Rs. 2½. The repeated issues of National War Bonds and subsequent Loans kept the presses busy with the printing of prospectuses, application forms, allotment letters, scrip, and finally the bonds themselves, while the consequent mass of new stock-holders multiplied by many times the work of producing dividend books and warrants. Treasury bills, both British and foreign, deposit certificates, currency note certificates and a host of other security documents, including the first issue of war saving certificates, piled Pelion on Ossa, and the shortage of space in which to work became more and more serious.

Once again, the authorities were faced with persistent applications from the Printing Office for more room. Sir Gordon Nairne, to whom as Chief Cashier these applications were made, once recalled that, some years previously, on the occasion of his receiving a similar appeal from the Principal of the Printing Office, he had been obliged to tell that official that if he wanted further space, he 'had better take the department up City Road'. It is not thought that Sir Gordon made this suggestion quite seriously; nevertheless, under the stress of war conditions, that is exactly what happened.

CHAPTER VII

ST LUKE'S PRINTING WORKS

THE STORY of how the printing department moved
'up City Road' is related fully by H. G. de Fraine
in his delightful book *The St Luke's Printing Works
of the Bank of England*, the sub-title of which reads 'An
Account, amongst other things, of the removal of the
Printing Department from Threadneedle Street and of its
establishment upon the Bank's Peerless Pool Estate[1] in
Old Street'. In this book, the author gives a description
of how this gigantic task was carried out, and of the difficulties with which he and his staff had to contend, but it
will be necessary, in order to complete our picture, to
recount some of the leading events.

It was in October 1915 that the Bank first heard that the
premises in Old Street, occupied by St Luke's Hospital,
were about to be vacated. Negotiations ensued immediately,
with the result that, a year later, the purchase was completed, and in April 1917, the Bank entered into possession.
F. W. Troup was entrusted with the conversion of the old
building, erected in 1782 to serve the purpose of a mental
hospital, into premises suitable for the accommodation of
a printing works. But the requirements of the Printing
Office could not wait, and while the conversion of the old
building and the construction of a machinery hall behind
it, were proceeding at the eastern end of the building, one

[1] The Peerless Pool was a swimming pool which, until 1869, lay
behind the hospital. The history of this pool, and of the pleasure gardens of which it was the principal attraction, is related in *The St
Luke's Printing Works of the Bank of England*.

143

section after another moved from the Bank into suitable, or, more often, unsuitable, quarters in the part that remained untouched. Here they carried on their work, the machinery being erected on wooden floors, then 135 years old, which had in many instances to be propped up from below in order that they might support the weight of the plant. Furthermore, the sections had frequently to move as the work of reconstruction approached their temporary quarters, and before it was completed some of them had been obliged to move several times. During the period of transition, the administrative staff made daily journeys 'up and down the City Road', in order to keep in touch with the building operations and with the work of their department, then proceeding in two places a mile apart, for St Luke's is exactly a mile away from the Bank,[1] a distance too great for the Chief Cashier, of whose department the Printing Office still formed part, to exercise control.

Consequently in 1919 a Supervisor was appointed as his representative.

The work of reconstruction was completed early in 1920. F. W. Troup had done a wonderful piece of work; without impairing the façade of the old building, he had equipped it with ferro-concrete floors, had inserted an additional story, and had provided three large machinery halls at the back of the building. Here was the space for which the Printing Office had always yearned, and to the responsible officials it was like entering into the promised land. Here they had at their disposal an area of 156,000 square feet instead of the 24,000 square feet into which they had been obliged to cram their work at the Bank. The pressure had, to some extent, been relieved by the removal in 1915 of

[1] The entrance hall of the old hospital was equipped with a board, showing, for the purpose of computing cab-fares, the distances to various points in the Metropolis, and on this board the distance to the Bank of England was shown as 1,760 yards.

XV. St Luke's Hospital in 1812

the section printing the dividend books and warrants to premises in Tabernacle Street, where they occupied an area of 33,000 square feet, but here at St Luke's was space not only for all the work detailed in the last chapter, but also room for expansion and for the provision of amenities to ensure the welfare of the staff. The section printing the dividend books and warrants then moved in from Tabernacle Street, and on 22 April 1920, the last load of printing office plant left the Bank.

During the hurly-burly attendant upon the removal to St Luke's, the Bank of England £1 note had not been forgotten. From time to time, further proofs of the miniature note, with Maclise's vignette instead of the design that preceded it, were prepared and submitted to H.M. Treasury, where this charming little plate-printed note met with the approval, not only of the Treasury officials, but also of the Chancellor of the Exchequer himself. The substitution of the Bank's note for the Treasury's currency notes then in circulation was, however, not just a matter of printing, but a financial operation of magnitude. The matter was discussed fully by the Committee on Currency and Foreign Exchanges, which met in 1918 under the chairmanship of Lord Cunliffe, and, although there was no indication that the change was imminent, it was thought that the Bank should not be unprepared. Accordingly, a part of the necessary equipment, fourteen plate-printing machines, was acquired from John Macdonald, one of a family long associated with bank-note printing. They were rotary machines, the engraved steel plates being bent to fit the cylinders. These plates, after inking, were wiped and polished by a web of calico rolled upon another cylinder; they printed a sheet only $15\frac{1}{2}$ inches by 17 inches, and many more machines would have been required before they could be used to print the entire issue. As things turned out, however, they were never called upon to perform that task, but a few years later they were most usefully employed upon the notes of the South African Reserve Bank, which the Bank had been called upon to print. These notes provided a severe test of printing skill. The plate-printed design on the front was pictorial, and was repeated, in reverse, on the back of the note so that the two pictures were in perfect register, a difficult task and one that tried to the full the capacity of the plate-printers. The steel plates were produced by transferring from an original master-plate, but not by Oldham's machine, which had been superseded by W. H. Chapman's transfer press, in which mechanical means produced the pressure that had formerly depended upon weight alone.

It had been suggested originally that the Bank's £1 note should be printed upon hand-made paper, but it was realised that it would be impossible to obtain a sufficient quantity of such paper to provide for the large number of notes that would be required. But in 1917, this difficulty was, in some measure, removed by the production by Messrs Portal & Co. of a type of paper which had not long been invented, known as mould-made paper. It will be remembered that the watermark of machine-made paper is impressed by the dandy roll upon the surface of the paper, but, during the manufacture of mould-made paper, the pulp is picked up from the vat by a cylinder bearing the design of the watermark, which is thus moulded into the actual substance of the paper. The pulp is not engine-sized, the paper being tub-sized after manufacture, and so successful is the whole process that the product is indistinguishable from hand-made paper, unless subjected to an expert test.

The larger sheet of paper produced by this process was an invaluable aid to mass production, which had become a

XVI. St Luke's Printing Works in 1925

necessity in view of the increased demand for documents of all kinds. The notes for Rs. 5, for example, which, when they were first introduced—they were smaller than the other denominations ($3\frac{3}{4}$ inches x 6 inches)—had been printed eight on a sheet by letterpress, were now printed twenty-eight on a sheet by offset-lithography, which was then coming more and more into use. This process, as its name implies, is effected by printing, not directly upon the paper, but on to an indiarubber blanket, which then sets off the print on to a sheet of paper. The process was used, at first, for printing upon tin plates, for which purpose the resilience of indiarubber made it especially suitable, but it was realised before long that is was equally suitable for printing upon paper. The fact that a zinc plate, the surface being suitably grained, could be used instead of a stone, and that such a plate, if sufficiently thin, was capable of being fitted round a cylinder, had led to the invention of the rotary offset press, in which an india-rubber blanket, fitted round a similar cylinder received the print and immediately set it off upon a sheet of paper carried on a third cylinder. The Bank had first acquired one of these machines in 1913; more were soon purchased, and it was upon one of them that King George V, on 18 December 1917, had printed the first Nominative War Bond during a visit that he had made to the Bank, accompanied by the Queen and Princess Mary. Although the old-fashioned letterpress printer regarded the new method with scorn—'What is it', one can remember hearing, 'but a glorified rubber stamp?'—it provided an extremely effective and speedy method of printing which was indistinguishable from letterpress. By 1921, when the printing works had settled down at St Luke's, a number of these machines were running, many of them printing the smaller denominations of the Indian currency notes.

Nearly 140 years had elapsed since the special committee appointed in 1783 had recommended that 'the notes be printed within this House', and, now that the printing works had left the shelter of that 'House' and established themselves at a distance of a mile away from it, the Bank had to consider by what means they could govern their outlying satellite. In 1921 a special committee had been appointed 'to report and advise on the finance, methods and administration of St Luke's', and, as a result of their recommendations, there was appointed in 1922 a Standing Committee of the Court of Directors, to be known as the 'Committee on St Luke's', who were to be responsible to the Governor and the Court of Directors for the conduct of St Luke's Printing Works. In their turn, the officials of the printing works were responsible to this committee, and thus the Chief Cashier, under whose benevolent sway the printing department had worked ever since its formation, relinquished his control. At St Luke's there was the usual change of nomenclature; the Supervisor appointed in 1919 became the Principal Supervisor, the Principals were renamed Supervisors, and the Cashiers' Store, from which incidentally the last of the sub-cashiers had departed thirty years before, was now renamed the Security Paper Store. In one respect St Luke's was very fortunate. Among the directors appointed to serve upon the Committee on St Luke's was Mr Arthur Whitworth, who had been a member also of the previously appointed special committee. Two years later, Mr Whitworth became chairman of the Committee on St Luke's, a position that he held for twenty years until his retirement in 1946, during which time he acted as guide, philosopher and friend to the officials who were so fortunate as to serve under his leadership.

The printing works had now settled firmly into the new

premises, and the work of every section was proceeding smoothly. The whole of the floor-space, which had seemed so generous, was now fully occupied, and when in 1924 it seemed that the Bank would be called upon before long to produce the notes for £1 and 10s., the old problem of shortage of space again loomed large on the horizon. In 1923 the postal order contract, which the Bank had held ever since 1881, terminated and was not renewed, a circumstance which released some welcome floor-space, but in 1925 it became necessary to devote a large area to the installation of photogravure machines in order to print a new note for Rs. 10, the appearance of the third series of the British currency notes having led to a demand from the Government of India for a note that should embody that process. The Bank's contract for the printing of the India currency notes was due to expire in 1929, when the new printing works in India would be in operation, but arrangements were made to expedite the production at St Luke's, and by dint of intensive work, the contract was completed early in 1928. But the valuable space thus secured would not suffice for the expected increase of work; it had been found necessary to extend the premises, and building operations had been proceeding for some time within the precincts of the printing works. In 1926 an additional machinery hall was built on all that remained of the garden of the old hospital; excavation provided a commodious strong room as well as a large paper store, and the erection of additional floors over the central machinery hall completed the extension, the area of the printing works having been thereby increased by some 20,000 square feet.

During the whole of this time, discussions had been proceeding with a view to determining the form that the new notes should take. The original idea of the notes, that

L

they should be miniatures of the notes for higher sums, was abandoned, and when the final proofs had been submitted and approved, the appropriate plant and machinery was purchased and erected. In 1927 printing started, and on 22 November 1928, the day appointed by the Currency and Bank Notes Act of that year for the 'Amalgamation of the Note Issues', the new Bank of England notes for £1 and 10s. were issued. These notes are still in circulation, and it is beyond the scope of this work to enter into the details of their manufacture or of the printing methods employed. Upon one feature, however, comment seems to be permissible, namely, the wealth of machine engraving to be seen on both of these notes, for we, who have witnessed the first steps of machine engraving at the beginning of last century, and have encountered repeated suggestions for its adoption in the years that followed, cannot fail to be particularly interested to see how, at last, it came into its own on the notes of the Bank of England.

In the meantime, the McPherson bank-note printing machines pursued the even tenor of their way, and turned out their daily quota of notes of £5 and upwards, printed from electrotypes produced in just the same way as were the first of their kind in 1855. It will be remembered that, when the system was introduced at that date, provision had been made for the replacement, when worn, of any of the nine separate electrotypes of which the relief block was made up. As copper is a comparatively soft metal, the 'pieces' had frequently to be replaced, more especially those in which fine lines appeared; the electrotype printing the vignette, for example, would seldom last for more than 500 reams. In 1925, however, very soon after chromium plating had become commercially possible, H. G. de Fraine was among the earliest in this country to appreciate the value of this process for the purpose of facing electrolytically printing plates engraved in recess. The rights of such a process were acquired and a chromium plating plant was installed at St Luke's. Among other uses to which the plant was put was the chromium facing of electrotypes, a process which enabled from 1500 to 2000 reams to be printed without the necessity of changing a 'piece'. The success of this innovation was due in no small measure to the skill of W. H. Hawkes, the metallurgical chemist of the printing works, but it was an inspiration to him to produce something even more lasting. His aim was to do away with the separate electrotypes, and to produce a solid printing block, all in one piece, which, because of its chromium facing, would be so hard wearing that replacement would be unnecessary. In 1933, he perfected this plan and produced a composite block of electrodeposited nickel which was subsequently faced with chromium. It is not possible to say what the life of one of these blocks might be, for their use was discontinued when the method of printing was changed in 1945, but records show that, up to that time, one block had printed 37,193 reams and still showed no signs of wear.

There is little more to be told of the notes of £5 and upwards, and that little tells of elimination rather than of development and progress. From time to time, as we have seen, the issue of notes of denominations that were no longer in demand had been discontinued, and, for this reason, the notes for £200 had been withdrawn from circulation in 1928. But in 1939 a more sweeping elimination took place, when the provisions of the Currency and Bank Notes Act of that year made unnecessary the issue of branch notes, and they too were discontinued, 'London' notes being issued by the branches in their place. More sweeping still, however, was the action of the Bank in 1943, when, with the concurrence of H.M. Treasury, it was decided no longer to issue notes of £10 and upwards, leaving the 'fiver' the only denomination still to circulate. There was no question of the notes for higher sums being out of demand; the discontinuation sprang from quite a different reason, which, as the Chancellor of the Exchequer explained to the House of Commons, was, apart from the simplification of the production and handling of the note issue, to 'provide an additional handicap for those who may contemplate breaches of exchange control and other regulations'.

In 1945 the paper of the 'fiver' lost its characteristic deckle edges, all four of which are now clean cut, while the change in the method of printing, adopted in that year, places the note itself beyond the scope of our history, which therefore comes automatically to an end. But the future historian, who will pick up the threads where we have dropped them will have ample material with which to begin his narrative; the evolution and the manufacture of the notes for £1 and 10s.; the measures taken to deal with the emergency of war, and the introduction, due to the inventive ability of S. B. Chamberlain and the technical skill of Portals Ltd., of the metal thread which now runs through the paper of every Bank of England note, ranking with watermarking and protective colouring as one of the three great security measures employed for the protection of the public. All this, and more that is still to come, will, it is hoped, one of these days be written, so that a later generation will be able to follow the further history of the Bank of England note, as we have followed its past since 1694 when, four days after the sealing of the charter, the Court of Directors ordered 'that the Running Cash Notes be printed'.

LIST OF WORKS CONSULTED

ACRES, W. MARSTON. *The Bank of England from Within.* 1931.

ANDREADES, A. *History of the Bank of England.* 1909.

Annual Register.

BESSEMER, SIR HENRY. *Autobiography.* 1905.

Bibliographical Society. *Dictionary of Booksellers and Printers,* 1726-1775. 1932.

BOLTON, A. T. *The Works of Sir John Soane.* 1923.

BRADBURY, HENRY. *Lecture to the Royal Institution.* 1856.

Britannia Quarterly (staff magazine of St Luke's Printing Works).

BRYAN, MICHAEL. *Dictionary of Painters and Engravers.* 1904.

BUSH, O. C. Article in *Britannia Quarterly.* November 1931.

Cambridge History of India. 1932.

Chambers's Encyclopaedia. New ed. 1950.

Chemical and Metallurgical Engineering. 1925.

CLAPHAM, SIR JOHN. *The Bank of England: A History.* 1944.

DART, JOHN. *History and Antiquities of the Cathedral Church of Canterbury.* 1726.

——. *History and Antiquities of the Abbey Church of St Peter, Westminster.* 1742.

DE FRAINE, H. G. *The St Luke's Printing Works of the Bank of England.* 1931.

——. Article in *Britannia Quarterly.* August 1921.

——. Article in *Old Lady of Threadneedle Street.* March 1924.

DENNISTOUN, JAMES. *Memoirs of Sir Robert Strange.* 1855.

Dictionary of American Biography.

Dictionary of National Biography.

EASTON, H. T. *The History of a Banking House* (Smith, Payne and Smith). 1903.

Encyclopaedia Britannica.

FEAVEARYEAR, A. E. *The Pound Sterling.* 1931.

FORSTER, JOHN. *The Life of Charles Dickens,* ed. J. W. T. Ley. 1922.

FRANCIS, JOHN. *History of the Bank of England.* 1848.

GIUSEPPI, J. A. Article in *Genealogists' Magazine.* September and December 1949.

GOSCHEN, THE RT. HON. G. J. Speeches to Chambers of Commerce of Leeds and London. 1891.

GRAHAM, W. *The One Pound Note.* 1911.

HALL, F. G. *The Bank of Ireland,* 1783-1946. 1949.

HECKSHER, E. F. 'The Bank of Sweden' in J. G. van Dillen, *History of the Principal Public Banks.* 1934.

Hoare's Bank. A *Record,* 1673-1932. 1932.

HOLDSWORTH, SIR W. S. *History of English Law.* 1938.

HOLT, SIR JOHN. *Report of the Causes determined by Sir John Holt from 1688-1710.* 1738.

HOLTZAPFEL, CHARLES and J. J. *Turning and Mechanical Manipulation.* 1843.

Household Words. 1850.

HUNTER, DARD. *Papermaking.* 1947.

Institution of Civil Engineers. *Proceedings.*

JERROLD, BLANCHARD. *The Life of George Cruikshank.* 1882.

KNIGHT, E. H. *Knight's American Mechanical Dictionary.*

London Directory.

London Gazette.

MACLEOD, H. D. *Theory and Practice of Banking.* 1875.

MALCOLM, C. A. *The Bank of Scotland,* 1695-1945. 1948.

MARTIN, J. B. *The Grasshopper in Lombard Street.* 1892.

Ministry of Education. *A Guide to the Educational System of England and Wales.* 1945.

MUNRO, NEILL. *History of the Royal Bank of Scotland.* 1928.

Old Lady of Threadneedle Street (staff magazine of the Bank of England).

Parliamentary Debates (Hansard).

PHILLIPS, MABERLY. *A History of Banks, Bankers and Banking in Northumberland, Durham and North Yorkshire.* 1894.

POLO, MARCO. *The Travels of Marco Polo.*

PORTAL, SIR WILLIAM, BT. *The Story of Portals Ltd. of Laverstoke.* 1925.

——. Article in *Britannia Quarterly,* November 1921.

PRICE, F. G. H. *The Marigold by Temple Bar*. 1902.

REES, A. *Rees's Cyclopaedia*. 1819.

RICARDO, DAVID. *The Works of David Ricardo*, ed. P. Sraffa, vols. I–IV. 1951.

RICHARDS, R. D. *Early History of Banking in England*. 1929.

Royal Commission. *Reports of the Commission for enquiring into the mode of preventing the Forgery of Bank Notes*. 1819-20.

Royal Society of Arts. *Journal*. 1854.

——. *Transactions*. 1840.

——. *Report of the Committee on the prevention of the Forgery of Bank Notes*. 1819.

SAUNDERS, P. T. *Stuckey's Bank*. 1928.

SMITH, ADAM. *The Wealth of Nations*.

SMITH, J. CHALONER. *British Mezzotint Portraits*. 1883.

STAUFFER, D. McN. *American Engravers upon Copper and Steel*. 1907.

STRUTT, JOSEPH. *Biographical Dictionary of Engravers*. 1785.

The Times.

TIMPERLEY, C. H. *Dictionary of Printers and Printing*. 1839.

TREVELYAN, G. H. *English Social History*. 1944.

VACHON, MARIUS. *Les Arts et les industries du papier en France*. 1894.

WATERSTON, ROBERT. *Early Paper Making near Edinburgh* (book of the Old Edinburgh Club, vol. xxv).

Webster's Biographical Dictionary.

WEITENKAMPF, F. *American Graphic Art*. 1924.

WOOD, SIR H. T. *A History of the Royal Society of Arts*. 1913.

ADDITIONAL SOURCES

All Saints, Sutton Courtenay, Parish of. Parish Registers.

St Andrew, Holborn, Parish of. Rate Books.

APPENDIX. PRINTED NOTES ISSUED BY
THE BANK OF ENGLAND

Notes for varying amounts, with the figures in manuscript, were issued from the beginning. The subjoined table shows the date upon which 'London' notes of each denomination were first printed and the date upon which they ceased to be issued.

The first issue of 'branch' notes was in 1826; they were discontinued in 1939.

	First printed	Discontinued
10s.	1928	Still in circulation
£1 (first issue)	1797	1821
£1 (second issue)	1928	Still in circulation
£2	1797	1821
£5	1793	Still in circulation
£10	1759	1943
£15	1759	1822
£20	1725	1943
£25	1765	1822
£30	1725	1852
£40	1725	1851
£50	1725	1943
£60	1725-45	Before 1803
£70	1725-45	Before 1803
£80	1725-45	Before 1803
£90	1725-45	Before 1803
£100	1725	1943
£200	1725-45	1928
£300	1725-45	1885
£400	1725-45	Before 1803
£500	1725-45	1943
£1000	1725-45	1943

INDEX

157

For EU product safety concerns, contact us at Calle de José Abascal, 56–1°, 28003 Madrid, Spain or eugpsr@cambridge.org.

www.ingramcontent.com/pod-product-compliance
Ingram Content Group UK Ltd.
Pitfield, Milton Keynes, MK11 3LW, UK
UKHW042209180425
457623UK00011B/111